Healing the
Codependent Heart

Healing the Codependent Heart

Douglas Dobberfuhl, M.S.

WALNUT SPRINGS PRESS

To all those that carry heavy burdens.
To the silent suffering chained by the past.
To those who believe they have to do all and be all in order
to find validation, love, and acceptance.

ACKNOWLEDGMENTS

This book includes insights from some very courageous brothers and sisters in the gospel. To you, I humbly give thanks. I have worked with you, walked with you, and witnessed your pain and suffering as you struggle to become free from the past. I have been so blessed to witness the Lord's tender mercies in your lives. You are living witnesses that miracles are real and happening every day.

I express gratitude to my friend and colleague Tamera Smith Allred, M.A. Her example, vision, and understanding of the gospel of Jesus Christ have made me a better person.

As always, my ongoing relationship with the good people at Walnut Springs Press continues to be a delight. To Amy Orton and Linda Prince—I can only hope that other authors could be so lucky as I have been in working with you. Your invaluable expertise, insightful vision, and supportive encouragement keep me wanting to write.

There are many giants whose shoulders I have leaned against in writing this book, including Tian Dayton, Charlotte Kasl, Stephen Wolinski, Charles Whitfield, Brenda Schaeffer, Mellody Beattie, Robert Burney, Pia Mellody, John Bradshaw, Myna Somers, and Claudia Black. Thousands have been inspired by your research and writings. I humbly add my name to that list.

There is one who has taught me more about true charity than anyone else, and that is my wife, Stephanie. At home, at work, with friends, or family, she remains a shining beacon for me of codependent sobriety and love.

Finally, and I want to be as respectful and reverent as I can be, I publicly thank Heavenly Father and His Only Begotten Son, Jesus Christ. I am ever learning how totally dependent I am on help from Heaven. I have felt and continue to feel Their perfect love, long-suffering, mercy, and compassion in my daily life.

TABLE OF CONTENTS

PART 1

INTRODUCTION

The Lord said to Abraham, "My name is Jehovah, and I know the end from the beginning; therefore my hand shall be over thee" (Abraham 2:8). My young friends, today I say to you that if you trust the Lord and obey Him, His hand shall be over you, He will help you achieve the great potential He sees in you, and He will help you to see the end from the beginning.

Dieter F. Uchtdorf (Uchtdorf 2006)

CHAPTER 1

SEEING THE PROBLEM

Janet hovered. She was wound tight inside. She had to stand behind her husband Mark when he was on the computer to make sure he wouldn't look at pornography. He had just gotten his temple recommend back, and she couldn't bear the thought of him losing it again.

"You don't have to stand behind me, Janet," Mark said. "I'm just doing some work for tomorrow's meeting."

"I just want to make sure . . ." she replied.

"Make sure of what? That I won't look at porn? We have a filter on the computer." Irritation seeped into Mark's voice.

"I know, but maybe you'll find a way around it."

Angry, Mark turned to face his wife. "So you are going to be my police? You're going to watch my every move to make sure I don't do something bad?"

"I just don't want you to relapse." There was fear in her voice.

Mark shook his head and got up to leave. "I need some air."

"Where are you going?"

"For a walk."

"Do you want me to come along?"

"No!"

Three minutes later Janet got in her car and slowly pulled out of the driveway. She had to make sure Mark didn't walk to the gas station down the road and buy an adult magazine. He just didn't understand. She was trying to help him. Their eternal marriage was on the line!

This may seem extreme, but it isn't. The fear of losing everything—one's marriage, one's spouse, one's temple blessings—can be overwhelming. It can push people to do things they might not ordinarily do. Janet even drove by Mark's office several times a day just to make sure he was "okay." She asked him to fire his secretary because she was skinnier and prettier than Janet. The last straw was when Mark went to a conference three cities away, and Janet showed up to make sure he wouldn't fall into temptation at the hotel. They ended up in therapy because he felt smothered and resentful of her actions. The more he pushed her away to get some space, the more she tried to get closer.

Janet is an example of someone who is codependent. It is what most people think of when they hear the term *codependency*—that someone is married to an addict of some sort and is exhibiting extreme behavior to control the addict. And most people would be right. Many spouses—men and women—can resort to codependent thoughts and behaviors when married to an addict. No one plans on marrying an addict. No one consciously seeks the kind of anguish that comes from loving someone who can't return that love.

Yet how does the individual get to that point? What else is going on within the person's inner life that supports codependent behavior? And what about those who are not married to addicts—can others exhibit codependent actions as well? What do latter-day prophets and Apostles teach us about this topic? How can the Atonement of Jesus Christ help someone overcome this problem? These questions and many others will be answered in this book.

Definitions of Codependency

Codependency is the bedrock or foundation for most maladaptive and addictive patterns of behavior. Yet it often lives in the blind spots of our lives, and as such, it can be hard to recognize, define, and diagnose. Let's review some definitions and get a clearer understanding of this label.

Definition #1

The prefix *co* in the word *codependency* refers to the connection between us and someone or something else. *Co* is attached to the word *dependency* to convey the understanding that our mental and emotional health is directly connected to and dependent on what other people are thinking and doing. We are acting codependently when we tell ourselves, "I will only be happy when my loved ones stop their addictive behaviors." If we are codependent, our happiness, peace, and stability are dependent on what our addicted loved ones are or are not doing, placing us in an emotionally vulnerable position. (Healing 2013, 16.)

Definition #2

Codependency is a compulsively reactive condition that is typically the result of growing up in an emotionally dishonest, spiritually hostile, and shame-based environment (Burney 1995, 5). In this environment, the child yearns to be loved and held and assured that everything is okay. As the child becomes an adult, he or she reaches out to others to try to save, fix, and/or take care of them. This is the codependent person's way of proving to himself or herself, and others, that he or she is needed, valuable, and worthwhile. In addition, the codependent individual offers help and support, makes great sacrifices, and gives incessantly. Codependents often overextend themselves, only to end up feeling emotionally and physically exhausted.

Definition #3

According to Weinhold and Weinhold, as children grow, they "complete a series of essential developmental processes. The two most important involve secure bonding between mother and child and the child's psychological separation from its parents" (Weinholt and Weinhold 2008, xi). Adult codependency occurs because there are deficits in these developmental processes. "When a person doesn't complete a developmental process, such as secure bonding . . . the need for completing it is carried along as excess baggage into the next stage of development . . . Codependent patterns repeat because they contain early developmental trauma that is unidentified and unhealed . . . it is, in reality, an attempt to heal" (ibid 5).

From these definitions, codependency can be summed up as the change that occurs when one has been wounded as a child and develops maladaptive coping strategies that are displayed in relationships. Think about an infant, all innocent and naive. As the little tyke interacts with this fallen, jaded, and dangerous world, he or she will get hurt. Everyone will, everyone does. Sometimes the wounding is done consciously, maliciously. Often, however, the wounding occurs simply because others in the child's life are imperfect.

As wounding occurs, the person's intellect, emotion, and spirituality become derailed and tainted. This altered state is called codependency. It is manifest in maladaptive internally based (inside of me) and externally based (outside of me) changes in behavior and ways of interacting with others. The goal of these changes is to overcome and heal from these wounds.

Codependency has several hallmark traits, which Pia Mellody details in her book *Facing Codependence* (2003). The following list of traits is adapted from that book.

- Difficulty with loving oneself. Prone to gossip; secretly jealous of others. Always comparing oneself to others. Struggles with self-pity and self-hatred.
- Difficulty protecting oneself. Can't say no and can't say yes. Can't handle confrontation or being assertive. Has trouble finding his or her voice when boundaries are violated. Often doesn't even know it is happening.
- Difficulty with self-care. Being overly needy—wants someone else to take care of him or her. Or being overly isolated—needless and wantless, there to serve others at the continual expense of one's own health. Constantly concerned with emotional and sometimes physical survival, these individuals were never able to learn proper self-care. Soothing, nurturing acts are foreign.
- Difficulty identifying who one is as a person, and struggling with how to share oneself appropriately with others. Outside of a relationship, the person feels lost, blank. His or her identity exists only within the relationship, the Church calling, the role he or she plays in the family. He or she may share too much information, or nothing at all. The individual has a habit of sharing himself or herself—becoming vulnerable—with people who are not safe or trustworthy.
- Difficulty experiencing and expressing one's reality in moderation. In other words, because codependent individuals have an inability to talk openly about their thoughts and feelings, they often end up displaying extremes—they are either over-the-top emotional or they are very analytical and unemotional.

What Codependency Looks Like—A General Snapshot

Generally speaking, a codependent person:

1. Is a people pleaser, rarely showing anger or offering a dissenting opinion.
2. Has difficulty with authority figures—is either too passive or too defensive around them.
3. Is prone to lying or exaggerating.
4. Tries too hard—is perfectionistic and compulsive.
5. Is able to be highly abstract in thinking (overly intellectual).
6. Is out of touch with own emotions, but highly sensitive to others' emotions—is a mirror to others' feelings.

7. Wants to help others—to save them and take away their pain. Goes to almost any length to accomplish that goal.
8. Has trouble with touch—is either too touchy or never touches at all.

Codependency causes a great deal of pain from unresolved wounds. It keeps us stuck in never-ending, exhaustive, and ultimately self-destructive patterns. The empty spots in our heart never get filled. Our self-esteem gets only momentary boosts—we are only as good as our last success. Our worth and value appear ever-changing.

Saving others, overextending ourselves, and creating intense emotional involvement are common behaviors for codependent people. Behind these actions are our subconscious goals to create confidence, feel powerful, be in control, be the center of attention, and believe we are wanted and desired. If these goals are met, anxiety is decreased and fear is lessened. These kinds of reactions and feelings are what the codependent person has always wanted, but could never produce on his or her own as a child.

A codependent's heart is like an empty cup that ends up being filled with other people's feelings. A codependent person's goal is to placate and decrease those strong emotions so he or she doesn't always feel overwhelmed and stressed out, so the cup doesn't overflow. Therefore, for a codependent to feel at peace, he or she needs to make sure everyone around him or her is at peace.

Codependency is a stumbling block to achieving true and lasting peace, having solid faith in God, and accessing the Atonement of Jesus Christ. It is an adaptive way of coping with life that promotes our wills, doing things our way, and generally managing life according to our own rules.

ASSESSMENT: AM I CODEPENDENT?

Take this assessment to see if you struggle with codependency. Answer yes or no to each question.

1. Growing up, were you not allowed to express emotions, or were you discouraged from doing so?
2. Growing up, were you not allowed to talk about problems, or were you discouraged from doing so?
3. Growing up, were you not allowed to rock the boat—to be your own person, or were you discouraged from doing so?

4. Growing up, were you treated as though love was conditional—based on performance?

5. Was there a lack of honesty in your family?

6. Do you find yourself being passive-aggressive?

7. Do you find yourself ruled by perfectionism?

8. Do you find yourself changing in order for others to feel comfortable?

9. Do you find yourself taking on the role of caretaker to the point that it defines who you are?

10. Do you struggle with seeing yourself as worthy and of value?

11. Do you struggle with respecting your boundaries and the boundaries set by others? Could you even define what a boundary is or looks like?

12. Do you struggle with accepting your thoughts, feelings, and personal perspective if others express differing opinions?

13. Do you struggle to own your needs—to know what they are and know when to ask for help?

14. Do you live and react in extremes?

15. Does your happiness depend on others around you being happy?

16. Do you step in to control or smooth over interactions that make you nervous? Do you get nervous around someone else's anger?

17. Do you say yes and make commitments when you really don't have the time or resources to follow through?

If you found yourself saying yes to many of these questions, this book is for you. Take heart. There is hope. There is a way to overcome this. The rest of the book will explore the root causes of codependency, why it has such a negative impact on our spirituality, and how to heal from it.

CHAPTER 2

DEPENDENCY

Since codependency is rooted in dependency, let's talk more about the meaning of this word. To be dependent on someone is to rely on him or her to get your own needs met. The dependent individual is influenced or controlled by someone else. He or she will take on a subordinate role within the relationship.

In childhood, dependence is a necessary part of human development. Indeed, it is built into the life cycle of most mammals, with humans exhibiting the longest period of dependence on their primary caregivers. An infant cannot meet his or her own needs. The dependent relationship offers the child safety, security, and an environment in which he or she can explore and learn. In healthy relationships, the primary caregivers nurture the dependent child with the goal of giving the child his or her independence as he or she is ready to manage and handle that independence. As there are so many different configurations of what a primary caregiver is (single mother or father, grandparents, foster parents, etc.), for the rest of the book I will simply use the term *parents* to refer to the person or persons who raised you.

Dysfunctional relationships with one's parents keeps the child in a dependent role. The focus is not so much to foster independence as it is to keep the dependency within the relationship to meet the needs of the parents. When I worked in a treatment facility for sexually abused teens, it was a common to hear female patients express the desire to become pregnant so they could have a baby that would love them and never leave them. In many instances, it sounded like the teenage girls could have been talking about getting a puppy. What was unrealistic was each of these young women wanted her baby to remain a baby. This might seem like an extreme example, but unfortunately it isn't. What the girls expressed was the secret desire many parents have as they create dependent relationships with their children.

Dependent children that remain stuck in this state are not allowed to grow and explore the world. There is usually a tight rein on behavior, with most choices made by one or both parents. Basic life skills are not taught to the child as he or she grows into adolescence. Some teenagers have confessed that they didn't know how to use a phone book, or read a bus schedule, or balance a checkbook. Sometimes the parent or parents will give the child money as he or she wants or needs it, without encouraging the child to develop work skills. Grown children leave home never having learned how to use a washing machine, empty a vacuum cleaner, or scrub a toilet.

In adulthood, the individual comes to rely on other adults to meet his or her needs, including emotional needs. Self-worth is built up by the other person. Fears and insecurities are left to the partner to deal with and manage.

In some instances, the wounded adult allows his or her partner to create a sense of self for the wounded person. The partner tells the codependent person what to eat, how to dress, where to go, how to act, etc. To be emotionally dependent on someone else as an adult is to give away one's autonomy, independence, and agency, or power to choose. This sets the person up to be needy and remain in a one-down, powerless position.

The other extreme is also common, where the codependent is needless and wantless. There is no dependency. Rather, the wounded adult has gone to the other extreme of not needing anyone. In this state, the person ends up using avoidant behaviors and will look to attach himself or herself to those who are dependent. This allows for the wounded adult to be in control and feel powerful within the relationship. Either way—dependency or avoidance— codependents struggle with themselves and how to connect to others in a healthy manner.

As stated previously, dependency is a natural state for a child. Peggy O'Mara believes that many adults were wounded because as children, their primary caretakers did not trust them to naturally grow and develop. Instead, the children were raised to see weaknesses, strong emotions, disasters, and being dependent on a parent as negatives in life instead of naturally occurring experiences. (O'Mara 1991, 55–59.)

Codependents often deny their own dependency needs—either unresolved from their own childhoods or within relationships as adults. Take the following quiz to help you see what dependency means to you and how you deal with this concept in relationships. Answer yes or no to these questions.

1. My needs were often ignored when I was a child.
2. As a child, I was pushed to become independent and autonomous before I was ready.
3. As a child, my emotions and perception of reality were ignored, downplayed, and even criticized.
4. As a child, I was expected to meet my parents' expectations and developmental timetable, instead of allowing my inner sense of time to regulate my growth.
5. As a child, if I expressed myself in a way different than what my parents' expectations were, I was punished in some way.
6. When I was a child, if I asked for help, my parents would become angry.
7. Growing up, there was nobody to go to when I was afraid.
8. Growing up, I was expected to take on the role of the third "parent" in our family.
9. As a child, if I acted silly or childish, I was criticized.
10. As a child, if I complained of not feeling well or was physically sick, my parents would get angry at me.
11. Growing up, I rarely received physical affection from my parents when I was ill, sad, or had experienced a failure. When these experiences would happen, my parents usually downplayed what I was feeling.
12. I do not like to discuss my needs with my partner.
13. I don't pay the bills—I let someone else do that.
14. I let someone else make the agenda of what needs to be done today.
15. I don't know what I want or need.
16. Others say I'm childish and needy.
17. Others say I'm too clingy.
18. I don't know where we keep the important papers, such as wills, car insurance, medical cards, etc.
19. I am afraid that my partner will get mad at me if I voice my needs.
20. To have needs is a sign of weakness.
21. I don't need to open up to others—I'm here for them, not the other way around.
22. I do not ask for help.
23. I keep my needs secret from others.
24. To be dependent means to be weak.

25. Depending on others means I will get hurt and let down.

26. I do not trust others to be there for me.

27. I confuse my needs with my wants.

The more you answer yes, the more you struggle with acknowledging your dependency needs, and the more you struggle with accepting yourself.

Spiritual development is the opposite of human development. It is to learn to become *more* dependent on the Lord, not less. It is to have our eyes opened to our human frailties and God's ultimate and perfect power. Humility, surrendering our will to His, being meek and lowly of heart—those are the attitudes the Lord desires us to cultivate.

Indeed, as we come unto Christ and are reborn, we become an "infant" in this new spiritual life. We have a new life, with the need to gain new skills and new knowledge and understanding. We are asked to change and become "as a child, submissive, meek, humble, patient, full of love, willing to submit to all things which the Lord seeth fit to inflict upon him, even as a child doth submit to his father" (Mosiah 3:19).

And we are safe in His arms.

CHAPTER 3
BEGINNING THE JOURNEY

The beginning of breaking the pattern of codependency is like going on a trip somewhere. You need to know where you are going, how to get there, and what to pack. So, let's look at each of these questions. First, where are you going? As an adult, having unresolved wounds (mental, spiritual, sexual, and/or emotional) from years past creates problems in the present. It creates codependency.

Struggles with intimacy, self-esteem, sexuality, addictions, keeping and maintaining relationships, and dealing with social situations are just a few of the stumbling blocks of codependency. That is where we are going—to overcome the past and reclaim the present with peace, strength, and confidence.

The second question is, how do you get there? As you read and do the exercises in this book, you will be able to define, reveal, and explore your childhood. Then, you will begin to see how the past influences your present-day problems, like a string moves a puppet. You will be able to work through, overcome, heal from, and truly let go of past wounds. You will learn new skills to help you move forward and maintain peace and serenity in your life.

The last question as you prepare for this journey of awareness and action is, what will you need to pack—take along—as you go forward? First, do not do this by yourself. The issues you will face may be emotionally charged and difficult to deal with. If left to our own thoughts, we can end up right back where we started. Ask for help. Do this with the guidance and help of your Father in Heaven. Remember, this is not a journey you can take by yourself.

If possible, get involved in the LDS Addiction Recovery Program. Use the twelve steps to help you overcome your codependency by applying the Atonement in your life. You will find support, strength, and understanding in those meetings.

Next, be gentle with yourself. There will be periods of great awareness as you progress, and with that awareness there may be periods of intense struggle. As this happens, take care of yourself. The process will take as much time as it needs to and will unfold naturally, organically—with Heavenly Father at the helm.

Find ways to soothe and comfort yourself that are not destructive. This may be a new idea, so experiment. Sometimes, even if you are an adult, you'll find a teddy bear can be very soothing, or snuggling up to a special blanket can be comforting. Don't be afraid to ask for priesthood blessings or go to the temple to seek out God's comfort. Remember that prayer can console our hurting and burdened souls: "Pray always, and I will pour out my Spirit upon you, and great shall be your blessing—yea, even more than if you should obtain treasures of earth and corruptibleness to the extent thereof. Behold, canst thou read this without rejoicing and lifting up thy heart for gladness? Or canst thou run about longer as a blind guide? Or canst thou be humble and meek, and conduct thyself wisely before me? Yea, come unto me thy Savior" (Doctrine and Covenants 19:38–41).

Be aware of your sleeping and eating habits. A lack of sleep—not enough, restless, or waking up and not being able to return to sleep—can impede your progress. Sleep problems can lead to irritability and depression, and can even trigger overeating or other addictions. You will need to plenty of sleep to deal with the strenuous emotional challenges ahead.

Review your eating. If you find yourself frequently eating fast food, cut back to once a week. Make sure you eat plenty of fruits and vegetables. Decrease your sugar intake. The healing process affects not just your emotional, mental, and spiritual life, but your physical body as well. You will need the energy to work through some tough issues. Having an exercise routine can also help you handle the stress you might encounter, or act as a way to work off stored resentments. Something as simple as a twenty-minute walk each day can do the trick.

Finally, no matter what happens, tell yourself, "I am okay. Right now, I'm okay." Life might be terrible for a while, so don't try to handle it all at once. Taking life apart and dealing with small bits is much easier to handle. A moment is easier to pass through than a day. Even if you struggle with your spouse, you're still okay. Even if you feel intense emotions, you're still okay. Even if things get worse before they get better, you're still okay.

God will use all of the resources at His command to help you leave the counterfeits the adversary has offered you, and bring you back into the arms of God's love. Robert D. Hales of the Quorum of the Twelve Apostles reminded us, "As we follow Him, He blesses us with gifts, talents and the strength to do His will, allowing us to go beyond our comfort zones and do things we've never before thought possible" (Hales 2012).

Truly, this journey of healing and overcoming codependency will take us out of our comfort zones. May we find comfort in the knowledge that Heavenly Father will bless us with gifts, talents, and strength. As we read in the LDS addiction recovery manual, "The Lord has all power. I'll relax and trust Him" (LDS 2005, 59).

CHAPTER 4

AGENCY AND AWARENESS

It is not easy to come unto Christ—to overcome a character weakness, or achieve sobriety from an addiction, or heal from some terrible trauma. Most of us struggle to change. We often make the same mistake over and over and over again, with little insight into why that behavior continues. Intervention often happens after the act is committed. Examples include:

- The alcoholic sobering up the next day and asking, "How did this happen again?"
- The elder's quorum president burning out because he doesn't know how to share the load with his counselors. He feels alone and overwhelmed and thinks about asking to be released . . . again.
- The mother who yells and loses her patience with her child for the umpteenth time, asking herself in anguish why she can't stop.

These are all examples of us using our agency—not unto salvation, but unto sin and bondage. Lehi counsels his sons not to "choose eternal death, according to the will of the flesh and the evil which is therein, which giveth the spirit of the devil power to captivate, to bring you down to hell, that he may reign over you in his own kingdom" (v. 29).

In that verse, Lehi teaches us all that when we use our agency from our fallen, natural state, "according to the will of the flesh," we will make choices that magnify the unenlightened, unchanged "evil which is therein." As King Benjamin taught, "For the natural man is an enemy to God" (Mosiah 3:19). When we use our agency from that natural state, we are, in essence, giving power to Satan to captivate us and put us in bondage.

The following are a few examples of what it looks like to use the natural man to manage life's problems:

- The overweight man who turns to ice cream instead of the Lord to manage his anxiety.
- The stressed-out boss who snaps and yells at his employees instead of turning to the Lord for help.
- The alcoholic who gets drunk to deal with his sense of loneliness and depression instead of trying to handle his profound sadness the Lord's way.

Character weaknesses that seem deeply entrenched in our personalities and countless addictions—these behaviors appear to rob us of our agency. They keep us floundering in sin and darkness. They keep us from reaching out to God. They keep us from becoming free—able to choose salvation. In other words, when we keep doing the same thing over and over, we will continue to get the same result. Drinking from a contaminated well will always give us stomach and intestinal problems. The key is to recognize that the well is dirty and contaminated, stop drinking from it, and then dig a new well.

Referring back to 2 Nephi 2:27, the beginning of that verse offers us hope—a new well, so to speak. Lehi teaches us that agency can give us the ability to intervene *before* we sin, allowing us to choose righteousness over sin, and therefore breaking free of the chains of hell. "Wherefore, men are free according to the flesh; and all things are given them which are expedient unto man. And they are free to choose liberty and eternal life, through the great Mediator of all men." This means that through (or because of, or as a result of) the Atonement of Jesus Christ, we are able to choose salvation. Through (because of) Christ, our agency does not bind us to Satan, but opens the door to heaven. And what is the gospel key that allows us to use our agency in such a manner? Repentance and coming unto Christ— becoming "a saint through the atonement of Christ the Lord" (Mosiah 3:19). Truly, without Christ, using our agency has the potential to damn us.

The first step in this journey is that of awareness, or as we learn in Primary, the first step of repentance is to recognize we've done something wrong. Becoming aware—learning truths that come from the Holy Ghost—helps us to see patterns and understand what is going on in our minds and hearts. Intervention (changing course) *before* we sin is now possible as more light and knowledge are given to us, thus allowing us to access the agency of salvation unto freedom from sin and bondage.

Personal awareness is a key element in obtaining the power to choose the right. Joseph Smith learned this lesson early in his ministry. It is a moment of Church history that many Saints are aware of, but I believe we often miss the point of the young Prophet's experience.

Martin Harris had been one of Joseph's scribes as the Prophet translated the Book of Mormon from gold plates. After Joseph had translated a portion of the ancient record, Martin begged the Prophet to let him show the written manuscript to a select few friends and family. After many prayers, Joseph let Martin take the 116 pages. They were lost, and Joseph lost the gift to translate for a period of time.

In Doctrine and Covenants 3, the Lord counsels Joseph. Listen to what He says:

> *And behold, how oft you have transgressed the commandments and the laws of God, and have gone on in the persuasions of men. For, behold, you should not have feared man more than God. Although men set at naught the counsels of God, and despise his words—Yet you should have been faithful; and he would have extended his arm and supported you against all the fiery darts of the adversary; and he would have been with you in every time of trouble. Behold, thou art Joseph, and thou wast chosen to do the work of the Lord, but because of transgression,* if thou art not aware thou wilt fall. *But remember, God is merciful; therefore, repent of that which thou hast done which is contrary to the commandment which I gave you, and thou art still chosen, and art again called to the work.* (vv. 6–10; emphasis added)

Let's apply this counsel in our own lives. It is a template or map of how to create change.

Step 1: See the problem. The Lord begins by telling Joseph what he did wrong—He states the reality of the situation to help Joseph see and understand what needs to change. Joseph was worried about saying no to Martin. Joseph allowed others to manipulate, coerce, and convince him to change his mind, to go against what he knew deep down inside was wrong.

Step 2: Understand that the problem can be overcome with God's help. The Lord then tells Joseph that he can stand tall, that he doesn't have to be afraid of what other people think or do. He reminds Joseph of His power. God's power, not Joseph's, is what needs to be reaffirmed. This is key. The Lord vividly describes how He would protect Joseph. These are words Joseph needs to believe and rely on in order to make the changes the Lord has commanded him to make.

Step 3: Build up confidence. The Lord also reminds Joseph who he is, which always helps to shore up sagging self-confidence and self-esteem. When faced or confronted with a mistake, we humans tend to initially see ourselves as less than and somehow less desirable. The adversary capitalizes on this reaction, and in many cases, he is the author of this view we adopt of ourselves. In these verses of Doctrine and Covenants 3, the Lord clearly shows us that His love for us, His own esteem of us, remains unchanged even in the light of our serious mistakes.

Step 4: Stay alert and create a "relapse plan." The Lord gives Joseph the following counsel: "If thou art not aware thou wilt fall" (Doctrine and Covenants 3:9). What should he be aware of? Joseph needs to remember this weakness in him. He needs to remain alert that this is an area that could prove dangerous in the future. He needs to be aware of his motives, his thoughts, and his secret or hidden fears and anxieties. As he remains open and vigilant, he will see things more clearly, to remember the eternal nature of the work he is called to, and that with God, all things are possible.

Step 5: Utilize the Atonement. The Savior then tells Joseph to repent—to change and work at overcoming this character weakness. He reminds the young Prophet that He is merciful and that He still wants to use Joseph and work with him.

The Lord said that if Joseph didn't become and stay aware, he would fall. This edict—to be aware—is one of the important truths we can take from his life. Indeed, in reviewing the life of the Prophet Joseph, we see that he remained ever humble and open to see weaknesses within himself. This character trait of his, humility, was key to his becoming and remaining aware of his internal world.

Awareness allows us to use our "agency unto salvation" because now we can see what we could not see before in our carnal states. We can see the patterns, secret or hidden motivations, and unspoken fears and insecurities that drive and motivate our behaviors. Maybe that is why the Lord commands us in Doctrine and Covenants 84:84 to "Live by every word that proceedeth forth from the mouth of God."

To review our discussion on agency and awareness, let's look at the following diagram.

"Captivity and death, according to the captivity and power of the devil" (2 Nephi 2:27).

"Choose liberty and eternal life, through the great Mediator of all men" (2 Nephi 2:27).

Using our agency from this state leads us to . . .

Using our agency from this state leads us to . . .

The carnal, fallen self. Going after our own wills—stubborn, prideful, full of fear, insecure.

Coming to Christ with a broken heart and contrite spirit. Be spiritually born again.

NATURAL MAN

CHRIST CENTERED

Let us follow the Savior's counsel to Joseph Smith. Let us become aware. And with that awareness, let us come unto Christ and use our agency unto salvation. Let us break the bonds of codependency. Let us become free of what fuels our codependent state—fears, resentments, poor self-esteem, and distorted beliefs about the past, present, and future. Truly, we can become free with God's help.

CHAPTER 5

TO BECOME ENLIGHTENED

Since seeing the problem is one of the biggest obstacles in healing from codependency, let's review a portion of Doctrine and Covenants 84. Here the Lord speaks again about awareness—discovering truth—and then how to apply that truth to become enlightened.

Verse 45: "For the word of the Lord is truth, and whatsoever is truth is light, and whatsoever is light is Spirit, even the Spirit of Jesus Christ." The truth of what we do and the patterns and triggers that promote our behaviors can be revealed to us through the Spirit. The Spirit gives us insight, an "inner sight" that allows us to make course corrections.

Verses 46–47: "And the Spirit giveth light to every man that cometh into the world; and the Spirit enlighteneth every man through the world, that hearkeneth to the voice of the Spirit. And every one that hearkeneth to the voice of the Spirit cometh unto God, even the Father." Here the Lord explains that the Spirit (the light of Christ) is given to every person who enters this world. This is akin to our conscience—our instinctive sense of right and wrong. Yet the blessing of becoming enlightened only comes to those that hearken (act according) to the voice of that Spirit.

Let's take the word *enlighteneth* apart to more fully understand this blessing. First, the prefix *en* means "to bring into the condition of." Then the next part of the word, *light*. And then the end of the word—*en*. As a suffix, *en* means the same thing as it does as a prefix—"to become or be made of." Put these definitions together and you get the following: to bring into the condition of light and become light, be made of light. That is what happens when we choose the right or use our agency unto salvation. We become filled with light, made of light. Our eyes are opened. We can see what we could not see before.

Verse 48: "And the Father teacheth him of the covenant which he has renewed and confirmed upon you, which is confirmed upon you for your sakes, and not for your sakes only, but for the sake of the whole world." As we open ourselves to more light, the Father teaches us the gospel, and more specifically, how to apply the Atonement to real-life situations and problems. This helps us to turn to the Lord with full purpose of heart, instead of the donut, the television, the video game, pornography, gossiping, etc.

Verse 49: "And the whole world lieth in sin, and groaneth under darkness and under the bondage of sin." It is true that the whole world groans under the weight of sin. Sin causes tremendous heartache and innumerable trials. Unless a person comes unto God, he or she will continue under the terrible weight of sin. No matter how hard we try, we can never find peace or freedom in darkness. The world's ways do not have the power to free us from darkness. The lie that I can have my cake and eat it too will never become true. It cannot be done. I cannot use worldly or carnal ways of escaping from grief or sadness and still expect to be a functional, spiritually whole person.

Verses 50–51: "And by this you may know they are under the bondage of sin, because they come not unto me. For whoso cometh not unto me is under the bondage of sin." It really comes down to listening to our conscience (the light of Christ) and seeking to become enlightened. If we still feel heavy and burdened down with life, and if we find hope to be elusive, it may be because we are trying to cope with life's problems ourselves—"because they come not unto me." To continue to manage life on our terms, we end up deceiving ourselves and others, attempting to minimize our consequences and rationalize our actions. It is the only way we can live in this state of incongruence—acting counter to or in opposition to the light of our conscience.

Verse 52: "And whoso receiveth not my voice is not acquainted with my voice, and is not of me." The Savior continues telling us that if we are not following Him, we become unacquainted with His voice (the voice of the Spirit) and are not numbered with the Saints. How many recovering addicts struggle with understanding the Spirit, struggle to understand and accept even the most basic spiritual doctrines? They have become unacquainted with the Lord's voice. Even the "regular" guy who stays home to watch football on Sundays eventually struggles to hear the voice of the Lord.

Verse 54: "And your minds in times past have been darkened because of unbelief, and because you have treated lightly the things you have received." Would it not characterize codependency to say, as it does in verse 54, that "[our] minds in times past have been darkened because of unbelief and because [we] have treated lightly the things [we] have received"? From a codependent point of view, the darkness of unbelief is how we secretly see ourselves, as not enough, not wanted, not good enough, not lovable. It is to struggle with the belief that God loves us personally and we don't have to do anything to convince Him that we are lovable.

Joseph Smith told us that we are darkened by unbelief and that light is restored as we come to have faith in God. To obtain this kind of faith requires us to learn the true nature of God.

> *Let us here observe, that three things are necessary in order that any rational and intelligent being may exercise faith in God, unto life and salvation.*
>
> *First, the idea that he actually exists.*
>
> *Secondly, a* correct *idea of his character, perfections and attributes.*
>
> *Thirdly, an actual knowledge that the course of life which he is pursuing is according to [God's] will. For without an acquaintance with these three important facts, the faith of every rational being must be imperfect and unproductive; but with this understanding it can become perfect and fruitful, abounding in righteousness, unto the praise and glory of God the Father, and the Lord Jesus Christ.* (J. Smith et al. 2010, Lecture 3; emphasis in original)

With childhood abuse (physical, sexual, and emotional), the concept of God becomes twisted and distorted. This often leads to future unbelief and blindness. This could be viewed as the darkness Joseph Smith spoke about—the misconceptions and lies about who and what God is. Without understanding the true nature of God, we will continue to use our own coping skills, our own ways of handling and managing life. For who can trust or offer up a contrite spirit to a God who is angry, selfish, and a liar (all attributes of those who hurt us as children)?

Joseph Smith explored six attributes of God in *Lectures on Faith*. These attributes, he explained, help us to trust God—to believe He will be there for us, believe He loves us and is approachable, and believe He will never lead us astray. Incorporated within these six attributes is a reminder of our relationship and connection to God—that He is the literal Father of our spirits. He is a perfect Father, full of wisdom, patience, long-suffering, compassion, and understanding.

> *First, that he was God before the world was created, and the same God that he was after it was created.*

Second, that he is merciful and gracious, slow to anger, abundant in goodness, and that he was so from everlasting, and will be to everlasting.

Third, that he changes not, neither is there variableness with him; but that he is the same from everlasting to everlasting, being the same yesterday today and forever; and that his course is one eternal round, without variation.

Fourth, that he is a God of truth and cannot lie.

Fifth, that he is no respecter of persons, but in every nation he that fears God and works righteousness is accepted of him.

Sixth, that he is love. (ibid)

The end of Doctrine and Covenants 84:54 talks about treating lightly the things we have received. As we are given knowledge and truth, many of us treat it lightly. As we are given truth, many of us ignore it. Light and truth bring us awareness, which many ignore, excuse, or treat as a thing of naught. We may be able to pontificate on gospel principles, emotionally healthy practices, or therapeutically sound processes, but if we don't live those principles, it is akin to treating lightly the insights and awareness given us by the Spirit. They sound good, and our intellect can make sense of them, but when we do not incorporate these truths into our hearts and our lives, behaviors don't change. We remain in darkness. In verse 55, the Lord calls this vanity, "which vanity and unbelief have brought the whole church under condemnation."

Pride (vanity) impedes us from acknowledging truth and discovering the patterns and processes that lead to sin, to repeating the past yet again, to acting out in addictions. We must understand these patterns in order to access agency unto salvation—to intervene before we get to the point of no return. If we choose not to put aside our pride (our vanity), the Lord declares that we are under condemnation until we repent of it.

Verses 56–57: "And this condemnation resteth upon the children of Zion, even all. And they shall remain under this condemnation until they repent and remember the new covenant, even the Book of Mormon and the former commandments which I have given them, *not only to say, but to do according to that which I have written"* (emphasis added). We are commanded to get congruent, which means that we do as we say and say as we do. The gospel is not only about teaching Sunday School lessons, but to live those lessons.

Verse 58: "That they may bring forth fruit meet for their Father's kingdom; otherwise there remaineth a scourge and judgment to be poured out upon the children of Zion." Let's make this verse more personal: "That [we] may bring forth fruit meet for [our] Father's kingdom; otherwise there remains a scourge and judgment to be poured out upon the children of Zion [us]." And what is the fruit the Lord is referring to? Repentance. A broken heart and contrite spirit. Obedience. Seeking to become enlightened. Becoming congruent, where our behavior matches our inner motivations.

Start today. Take a step toward becoming enlightened—to being filled with light. Make a single choice to try to live today according to the Lord's will. Seek for enlightenment. Pray for awareness. Use your agency unto salvation.

PART 2

The Spiritual View of Codependency

*Spirituality is a lens through which we view life and
a gauge by which we evaluate it . . . To be spiritually
minded is to view and evaluate our experiences in terms
of the enlarged perspective of eternity. . . . Elder John
A. Widtsoe taught that "there is a spiritual meaning of
all human acts and earthly events. . . . It is the business
of man to find the spiritual meaning of earthly things.
. . . No man is quite so happy . . . as he who backs
all his labors by such a spiritual interpretation and
understanding of the acts of his life" (in Conference
Report, Apr. 1922, pp. 96–97).*

Dallin H. Oaks (Oaks 1985)

CHAPTER 6

THE FALL AND CODEPENDENCY

Growing up with wounds from the past creates a state of general dysfunction called codependency. Codependency is the foundation for many forms of maladaptive coping/survival skills and addictive patterns of behavior. Take away the alcoholism, and the alcoholic will still be left with codependency. Scratch away the surface from a sex addict and you'll find codependency. Lock the fridge for a compulsive overeater and you'll still have codependency to chew on.

The LDS addiction recovery manual echoes this idea: "Your thoughts, feelings, and beliefs are actually the roots of your addictive behaviors. Unless you examine all your tendencies toward fear, pride, resentment, anger, self-will, and self-pity, your abstinence will be shaky at best . . . your addiction is a symptom of other 'causes and conditions' (Alcoholics Anonymous [2001], 64)" (LDS 2005, 21).

Codependency is the building block that creates a foundation for jealousies, anxieties, pride, avoidance, and doubt. These massive stumbling blocks are hewn from the great and endless quarry of misery, fear, abandonment, and rage. Codependency, then, is man's own way of coping or surviving in this dangerous, fallen world.

From the time Adam and Eve fell and left the Garden of Eden, the fallen world is graphically described in the scriptures. Enoch explained that because of the fall of Adam, "we are made partakers of misery and woe . . . And men have become carnal, sensual, and devilish, and are shut out from the presence of God" (Moses 6:48–49). Lehi taught the same lesson to his son Jacob: "[T]hat they [all mankind] were lost . . . fallen" (2 Nephi 2:21–22).

The Fall introduced the world to some very harsh conditions. Our natures, if left unchecked, will react just as harshly to this uncertain environment. Our fallen nature is blind, constantly reeling and reacting, and confuses the act of survival with actual living. In this state, we have forgotten our eternal nature and the plan of our Father in Heaven. We struggle to see or recognize our worth and value. Until we are spiritually reborn by applying the Atonement of Jesus Christ in our lives, our nature will continue to try to manage and control this fallen world alone. Self-will, pride, lies, and a host of sins and dysfunctional patterns become the tools for the fallen man and woman.

The following chart reflects the progression from birth to codependency:

1. The Seeds of Codependency

Being born into a mortal, fallen world. Life of the natural man or woman. Self-will in charge to handle stress, anxiety, fear, anger, loneliness. Trouble with trust, faith, and love. Unbridled living: physical body rules spirit. Families are imperfect, with members' weaknesses impacting each other negatively. Struggle with attachment, bonding, separation, independence.

2. Becoming Codependent

Living an externally based life (focusing on others—what is occurring outside of me rather than my own feelings, thoughts, needs). Maladaptive coping skills (handling daily life using techniques that are counterproductive in the long term). Living with blind spots, denial, ingrained patterns of thought and behavior, and unacknowledged wounds. Living with triggers that promote extreme reactions.

3. Distraction and Escape

Addictions (food, spending, sex, drinking, drugs, etc.), compulsive acts (three hours on Facebook a day, hobbies, etc), getting "lost" in a project—unable or unwilling to act in moderation.

4. End Result

Emotionally and spiritually disconnected from God, self, and others

The devil is the author, director, and teacher of the fallen. Therefore, even in our best moments, as long as we remain in our carnal, fallen state, we will always find his shadow in our lives. He is the creator of many of our sufferings. He is the mastermind behind our childhood abuse. Knowing the psychology and biology of trauma, Satan works endlessly to wound us emotionally and mentally. He understands our earthly developmental process and seeks to disrupt and derail it. He recognizes that to sow the seeds of future sin—future spiritual stumbling blocks—he needs to start early.

And then what does the author of sin do? He gives us the manual of how to manage, deal with, and control all those memories, all that dysfunctional baggage. He sells us the medicine that will soothe our wounds—the very ones he gave us. He tells us how great we are because we did twenty-five hours of service at church this past weekend, even though we had to be away from our family. We get pats on the back—people laud us as the great workers in the ward. So why does our spouse come to resent us, and our children seem distant? Don't they know we are doing the work of the Lord? Yes, the adversary is most cunning.

Satan has an unquenchable thirst for power and constantly seeks revenge against his Father. How does he do that? He attacks the very thing his Father loves most—His children. The devil wants all of his spirit brothers and sisters that chose to follow God and Christ in the pre-earth life to be miserable. Satan fosters misery by whispering lies, encouraging survival using his tools, and twisting truth.

Even if we are unaware (subconsciously or covertly) that we are implementing these counterfeit tools of happiness and peace, the result is the same. We may desire to be good, to do good, and to follow God. We may not purposefully or maliciously try to hurt ourselves or others, yet when we act from a codependent state, the end result is the same. Dealing with this fallen world—trying to find safety, peace, and security any other way than God's way—will eventually bring us misery, exhaustion, hopelessness, bitterness, resentment, and impatience.

Satan is sly and subtle, full of trickery and deceit. He never stops. He's constantly disseminating his propaganda. He'll use our fears and insecurities against us, magnifying them and telling us that our over-the-top reactions are justified. Our need to do it our way, to control the situation, is the only way things will work. When we get together to plan Relief Society lessons and activities, we have to push our agenda, squashing any dissenting opinions. When we go to church, the kids had better behave or other members in the congregation will look at us and whisper about how terrible we are.

Satan will remind us over and over of our sins and shortcomings, telling us that we are worthless. And the only way to get back some of that worth? Be good. Be really, really, really good. High expectations will do the trick (even though in truth they are unrealistic expectations). You have to prove to Jesus and Heavenly Father that you are worth loving. Endless good works and rigid obedience outweigh mercy, compassion, love, and forgiveness.

Remember how Lucifer became the devil. In (Moses 4:3–4), the Lord explains that "Because . . . Satan rebelled against me, and sought to destroy the agency of man, which I, the Lord God, had given him, and also, that I should give unto him mine own power; by the power of mine Only Begotten, I caused that he should be cast down. And he became Satan, yea, even the devil, the father of all lies, to deceive and to blind men, and to lead them captive at his will, even as many as would not hearken unto my voice." President Marion G. Romney echoed this scripture by stating, "Satan's methods are various, devious, and countless" (Romney 1971). And President Joseph F. Smith declared:

> *Let it not be forgotten that the evil one has great power in the earth and that by every possible means he seeks to darken the minds of men and then offers them falsehood and deception in the guise of truth. Satan is a skillful imitator, and as genuine gospel truth is given the world in ever-increasing abundance, so he spreads the counterfeit coin of false doctrine. Beware of his spurious currency, it will purchase for you nothing but disappointment, misery, and spiritual death. "The father of lies" he has been called, and such an adept has he become, through the ages of practice in his nefarious work, that were it possible he would deceive the very elect.* (J. F. Smith 1948, 20–21)

As the chief architect of this fallen world, Satan urges us to accept lies as truth—to see evil as good. He truly is the great counterfeiter. The devil is focused on peddling his merchandise to us, the members of the Lord's kingdom here on earth. Satan wants to replace the pure, real, authentic, eternal, heaven-sent guidance and truth with his knockoffs and fakes.

Satan knows it is easy for a stalwart member of the Church to reject something filthy. But when the unclean is dressed up and made to appear as good as the real thing, suddenly it becomes easier for even the most solid Saints to accept it. Sister Lee Ann Peterson, one of my adult Sunday School teachers, offered the class the following example of this concept.

> *In 1899, Brigham Young asked the Cache Valley Saints to build a road through Logan Canyon to the Bear Lake Valley. During this construction, a spring was*

discovered, which came to be called Ricks Spring. It was very popular. It was a great place for canyon travelers to stop, stretch, and enjoy the ice-cold water. Many even took home jugs of the water.

In the 1950s, hydrologists noticed that there was a connection between Ricks Spring and the Logan River. The Logan River is filled with fish, beavers, ducks, geese, muskrats, deer, and moose. However, it wasn't until 1972 that a terrible discovery was made. The water from Ricks Spring actually came from three different sources: the Logan River, the Tony Grove Lake, and a livestock camp higher up the mountain.

From the beginning, people would sometimes get digestive ailments when going through the canyon. Now an explanation was found—those who drank from the spring were actually drinking filthy, contaminated water. No matter how clear or ice cold it was, or how good it tasted, the water from Ricks Spring was filled with contaminants. (author's unpublished notes, October 2010)

One of the greatest lies, one of Satan's best counterfeits, is to portray codependency as charity. Why? Because he wants us to use our survival skills and character weaknesses to manage life. We think we're doing the right thing, yet the more we try to be a good Latter-day Saint from this state, the more frazzled and exhausted we become. We wonder how people can get up in testimony meeting and speak so personally about feeling God's love. We wonder why we can't feel the blessings of the Atonement. One sister said, "I grew up in the Church. I went through Primary and Young Women and got married in the temple. I do everything right. I am always there, always serving. But if you asked me if I have a personal relationship with the Savior, I'd have to say no. I'm living an intellectual testimony. I don't think I've ever felt God's love for me."

Therefore, it behooves us to try to better understand what true charity looks like. In general conference, Aileen Clyde reflected on charity—what it is and what it is not. She addressed many of Satan's counterfeits that make up codependency: "It is not charity or kindness to endure any type of abuse or unrighteousness that may be inflicted on us by others. God's commandment that as we love him, we must respect ourselves, suggests we must not accept disrespect from others. It is not charity to let another repeatedly deny our divine nature and agency. It is not charity to bow down in despair and helplessness. That kind of suffering should be ended" (Clyde 1991).

The following chart compares charity and codependency, breaking down the attributes of charity and their counterfeits. See if you can find any of these examples in your life.

TRUE PRINCIPLE—CHARITY	SATAN'S COUNTERFEIT—CODEPENDENCY
And charity suffereth long (patiently enduring wrongs or difficulties, patient endurance)	Denial, minimizing, normalizing abusive acts done to us. Swallowing our needs and wanting to make life easier for others. People pleasing.
and is kind	Enabling others—not holding them accountable. Not placing boundaries or limits on others' behaviors. ("That is mean.") Doing for others what they can and should do for themselves.
and envieth not (not feeling a jealous or somewhat admiring discontentment at the possessions, achievements, or qualities of another; not desiring to have for oneself something possessed by another)	Compartmentalizing these secret desires and motivations. Seeking to match or "top" what others are doing. Driven to be the best, to outshine, outperform, outserve, and outlive the gospel in your congregation and family.
and is not puffed up (not prideful)	Being judgmental, seeing self as better than OR as less than. Always comparing. Bragging about spouse's/child's/parents' accomplishments.
seeketh not her own (not selfish)	Being helpful and nice with a secret intent for the other person to meet your needs. "I scratch your back, you scratch mine" attitude. Keeping the peace for own self-interest (safety, self-esteem boost, control, looking powerful). Playing the role of victim or martyr.
is not easily provoked (not easily incited to anger or resentment)	Squashing any feelings of anger. Always smiling. Always stuffing any kind of displeasure. Holding resentments is okay as long as they stay buried.
thinketh no evil	Secretly applauding another's failure. Gives us a feeling of one-upmanship, feeding off of our poor self-image. Judging silently. OR seeing the plight of others and coming to the rescue: "I will save you from the evil. Here, let me pick up all your baggage you've accrued over the years."

and rejoiceth not in iniquity	Whitewashing, minimizing, normalizing, encouraging blind spots. "I'll do more than that—I won't even see or acknowledge iniquity, especially if it's in my own home." OR "You made your bed, now sleep in it. This is your problem and you can drown in it."
but rejoiceth in the truth	Basing truth on what I see—my perception, going through my filter. Therefore, truth is often distorted. "I rejoice that I came from a very put-together family (even though Dad was a workaholic and Mom was always competing with her best friend and I felt emotionally abandoned, but let's not look at that)." OR "Jenny, you really need to go on a diet. You have really let yourself go. What? I'm just telling her the truth. I'm pointing it out to her because I'm her friend."
beareth all things	Being needless and wantless. Suffering silently. Fear of standing up for self, fear of being rejected, fear of being discounted. OR "I am Superman/woman. I'll watch our kids, make dinner for Sister Rogers because she just had a baby, sew our daughter's dress for the recital, take Bobby to soccer practice, help James with his book report, and clean the house before you bring home your client, all in the next three hours."
believeth all things	Being naive, turning a blind eye, enabling others. "Oh, you don't know how the porn got on our computer? Okay, I believe you."
hopeth all things	"Even though all signs point to the contrary, and there are very clear patterns at work, I hope Bethany doesn't go drinking tonight. I won't say anything, just hold my breath and cross my fingers."
endureth all things (Moroni 7:45).	Acting the victim/martyr role. Not standing up for yourself. Just taking it. OR doing it all by yourself.

CHAPTER 7

REPENTANCE AND CODEPENDENCY

"But I'm not committing a sin. Why do I need to change? Why do I need to repent? Why should I seek godly sorrow? I'm not getting drunk, or high, or having sex with someone else. I just have some codependency issues."

The person who thinks that doesn't fully understand the seriousness of codependency—the hidden motivations, the overemphasis on behavior, and the false fronts created by codependent individuals. In general conference, Elder Lynn G. Robbins declared:

> *To be and to do are inseparable. As interdependent doctrines they reinforce and promote each other. Faith inspires one to pray, for example, and prayer in turn strengthens one's faith.*
>
> *The Savior often denounced those who did without being—calling them hypocrites: "This people honoureth me with their lips, but their heart is far from me" (Mark 7:6). To do without to be is hypocrisy, or feigning to be what one is not—a pretender.*
>
> *Conversely, to be without to do is void, as in "faith, if it hath not works, is dead, being alone" James 2:17; emphasis added). Be without do really isn't being—it is self-deception, believing oneself to be good merely because one's intentions are good.*
>
> *Do without be—hypocrisy—portrays a false image to others, while be without do portrays a false image to oneself.* (Robbins 2011; emphasis in original)

Let's review the two realms where codependency can cause some real problems—our inner motivations *(to be)* and our outward acts *(to do)*. This will help us gain a better sense of what is really happening when we live in a codependent state.

INNER MOTIVATIONS

The Book of Mormon speaks very clearly about this issue. At the beginning of his great discourse on faith, hope, and charity, Mormon talks about inner motivations and secret desires. This important truth is often unseen or disregarded when studying this chapter of the Book of Mormon. To gain charity, the pure love of Christ, we need to be aware of our inner state of being—why we do what we do. Part of codependency is about focusing on outward manifestations of good works—building and forming a front, a mask, a façade for others. Mormon states: "For behold, if a man being evil giveth a gift, he doeth it grudgingly; wherefore it is counted unto him the same as if he had retained the gift; wherefore he is counted evil before God" (Moroni 7:8).

Mormon goes on to say that a bitter fountain cannot bring forth good water. Those who do good works are of God. Those who do evil works are of the devil. But what about those who do good works but whose hearts are not broken and whose spirits are not contrite? Mormon states simply, "It profiteth him nothing, for God receiveth none such" (v. 9).

Indeed, there is no healing in empty works, no matter how many are performed. An excommunicated member, struggling to repent and return to the Church, told me, "Won't it be enough if I do lots of service? If I can't leave my sex addiction—if I can't repent—then at least my works should account for something."

I sadly shook my head. "No, good works are not enough. You must be baptized to return to your Father in Heaven. No amount of good works and selfless service can take away that requirement. In the end, it will profit you nothing. You must seek out a broken heart and contrite spirit. You must get real and honest with yourself and God."

The LDS addiction recovery manual states: "In the past, if you were religiously active, you may have been motivated by fear of the judgment of God or of what others would think. Perhaps you acted out of a sense of duty . . . Consider whether your activity in the Church is still motivated by fear or duty or if it is a natural outgrowth of your reborn faith in Christ" (LDS 2005, 54).

Most codependents are very busy people, trying to help others. However, whether they know it or not, the true motivation for many people struggling with codependency is managing their fear and insecurity. As recorded in Moroni 7, charity can't be achieved without first reflecting on our thoughts and intents and reasons—what it is that actually drives us to act.

Will I help Sister Brown move into a nursing home because I feel guilty and embarrassed if I don't show up to visit her? Do I rake Brother Smith's yard, but grumble the whole time under my breath? Do I say yes to yet another project at church even though I don't have the time, and come to resent the assignment? Do I ever start to see Church membership as a burden? Or am I always giving, giving, giving, and so excited for opportunities to serve, but inwardly believe I am a worthless piece of trash? Do I hate myself so much I can't look at myself in the mirror? Maybe I can prove I'm not garbage if I do all my home teaching or visiting teaching.

Linda K. Burton, Relief Society general president, counseled us to reflect on our true motivations and ask, "'Am I doing this for the Savior or am I doing this for me?' That way, our service will more likely resemble the ministry of the Savior" (Burton 2013).

OUTWARD ACTS

King Benjamin taught that "when [we] are in the service of [our] fellow beings [we] are only in the service of [our] God" (Mosiah 2:17). However, codependency interprets this scripture as a license or edict to do all and be all. Service becomes the great measuring stick, letting us and everyone else know how good we are.

As this Book of Mormon prophet continued his great discourse, he made it clear that service is connected to gratitude. The more we can see the hand of the Lord in our lives, recognizing the blessings that flow to us daily from Him, the more grateful and humble we will be. From this place of humility and gratitude, service becomes a natural outgrowth, a natural reaction. This is what Mormon was getting at—charity comes from a place of humility and gratitude.

Charity does not bear the fruits of being emotionally exhausted, drained, stressed out, overextended, overwhelmed, bitter, resenting doing good works, or seeing oneself as unappreciated. These are the fruits of codependency. No matter how hard we try, no good can ever come from living and operating from a state of codependency.

In contrast, the fruits of charity are love, meekness, loyalty, respect—in other words, coming to think and act as the Savior does, having our perspectives aligned with His. We come to have, as Alma said, "the image of God engraven upon [our] countenances" (Alma 5:19).

King Benjamin and Mormon knew that this journey in life—the journey of turning to Christ and adopting His ways to manage this fallen world—was a process, a line-upon-line experience. That is why the following words of caution were uttered: "And see that all these things are done in wisdom and order; for it is not requisite that a man should run faster than he has strength. And again, it is expedient that he should be diligent, that thereby he might win the prize; therefore, all things must be done in order" (Mosiah 4:27).

The goal is not to make this change as quickly as possible. It is not about the speed at which we run the course. The goal is to endure. This journey of letting go of the things of this world for the things of heaven is at times grueling, stretching, and even painful. Replacing codependency with charity is akin to applying Christ's Atonement to your self-esteem problems, or to unresolved childhood abuse, or to your fears of intimacy. Speed doesn't matter. Perfection is not the current goal on earth. No, it is to keep on keeping on—to get back up when we stumble, to try and try and try at implementing these new skills, beliefs, and ways of living. Reflect on Nephi's words:

> *Wherefore, do the things which I have told you I have seen that your Lord and your Redeemer should do; for, for this cause have they been shown unto me, that ye might know the gate by which ye should enter. For the gate by which ye should enter is repentance and baptism by water; and then cometh a remission of your sins by fire and by the Holy Ghost.*
>
> *And then are ye in this strait and narrow path which leads to eternal life; yea, ye have entered in by the gate; ye have done according to the commandments of the Father and the Son; and ye have received the Holy Ghost, which witnesses of the Father and the Son, unto the fulfilling of the promise which he hath made, that if ye entered in by the way ye should receive.* (2 Nephi 31:17–18)

This is the moment of rebirth, the beginning of our new life, as new creatures in Christ. We have been washed clean of the Fall. We have left the carnal world. We have buried the natural man—the old man of sin, as Paul says—and come up out of the waters of baptism as new individuals. But this newness requires us to learn new skills and develop new talents. Nephi counsels us to not sit back and relax, thinking this birthing experience we have gone through is the end of the journey.

> *And now, my beloved brethren, after ye have gotten into this strait and narrow path, I would ask if all is done? Behold, I say unto you, Nay; for ye have not come thus far save it were by the word of Christ with unshaken faith in him, relying wholly upon the merits of him who is mighty to save.*
>
> *Wherefore, ye must press forward with a steadfastness in Christ, having a perfect brightness of hope and a love of God and of all men. Wherefore, if ye shall press forward, feasting upon the word of Christ and endure to the end, behold, thus saith the Father: Ye shall have eternal life.* (vv. 19–20)

Yes, these new skills will not come easy and will not be mastered after only a few attempts. Keep going, keep trying, and never give up. Trust in Jesus Christ and Heavenly Father. Foster spiritual hope that comes from the Holy Ghost, not from yourself. Read the scriptures, study the general conference talks, and then attempt to implement those truths into your daily life. And then keep trying, keep repenting, keep turning back to Christ. After all, is this not what enduring to the end looks like? Is this not what the daily struggle is—to maintain this new life, this new birth, and slowly mature to become like the Savior? "That when he shall appear we shall be like him, for we shall see him as he is" (Moroni 7:48).

CHAPTER 8

THE HEART OF CODEPENDENCY—
DESTROYING AGENCY

The prophet Alma offered what I believe is the greatest scriptural sermon on codependency and its harm to the soul. Of course, he didn't say the word *codependency*, as it didn't exist at the time, but the idea and intent are the same. Let's study and reflect on his words.

> *O that I were an angel, and could have the wish of mine heart, that I might go forth and speak with the trump of God, with a voice to shake the earth, and cry repentance unto every people!*
>
> *Yea, I would declare unto every soul, as with the voice of thunder, repentance and the plan of redemption, that they should repent and come unto our God, that there might not be more sorrow upon all the face of the earth.* (Alma 29:1–2)

Alma has good intentions—he wants everyone to be at peace, and he wants to rid the world of sorrow. This is a snapshot of what codependency can look like for Latter-day Saints. Yet Alma censures himself pretty harshly in the next verse for thinking this way:

> *But behold, I am a man, and do sin in my wish; for I ought to be content with the things which the Lord hath allotted unto me.* (v. 3)

In the next few verses, Alma reminds himself why what he wanted was sinful. Here we see one of the most destructive consequences of codependency: the slow and steady destruction of another's agency.

> *I ought not to harrow up in my desires the firm decree of a just God, for I know that he granteth unto men according to their desire, whether it be unto death or*

unto life; yea, I know that he allotteth unto men, yea, decreeth unto them decrees which are unalterable, according to their wills, whether they be unto salvation or unto destruction

Yea, and I know that good and evil have come before all men; he that knoweth not good from evil is blameless; but he that knoweth good and evil, to him it is given according to his desires, whether he desireth good or evil, life or death, joy or remorse of conscience. (vv. 4–5)

In these verses, Alma reflects on agency. He wanted to have the power to cause everyone to receive salvation (speaking with the trump of God, shaking the earth—not unlike what Alma himself experienced when an angel appeared to him). God decreed, Alma reminds himself, that men are free to choose according to their wills and to receive the consequences of their choices.

Codependency erodes agency. Codependency builds an illusion of being powerful and in control, based on a lack of respect for other people's agency. Without control, codependency whispers, there is more fear. And fear is what codependency tries to manage most. Managing fear pushes the codependent to overstep bounds, to do more for others and to others.

Now, seeing that I know these things, why should I desire more than to perform the work to which I have been called?

Why should I desire that I were an angel, that I could speak unto all the ends of the earth? (vv. 6–7)

Alma asks himself, "Why should I overstep my bounds? Why should I want more than what is within my sphere of influence and responsibility?"

For behold, the Lord doth grant unto all nations, of their own nation and tongue, to teach his word, yea, in wisdom, all that he seeth fit that they should have; therefore we see that the Lord doth counsel in wisdom, according to that which is just and true. (v. 8)

Here, Alma reminds himself that the Lord calls people of each nation to preach His gospel. Alma doesn't have to, and can't, teach all of the people himself.

I know that which the Lord hath commanded me, and I glory in it. I do not glory of myself, but I glory in that which the Lord hath commanded me; yea, and this is my glory, that perhaps I may be an instrument in the hands of God to bring some soul to repentance; and this is my joy. (v. 9)

Healthy Motivations

After checking his thoughts and motivations in the previous verses, Alma recognizes that it is good to desire to be an instrument in the hands of the Lord. In the next three verses, Alma states over and over how he remembers his captivity and the captivity of others, and how only God was powerful enough to deliver them. This remembrance fosters humility in Alma, and here we see the key to healthy motivations: humility, humility, humility. Alma will do nothing other than what God wants him to do. This prophet will not forget where he has been and how the Lord rescued him from sin. Alma knows he is no better than anyone else. He waits upon the Lord. Alma is not a man who seeks power or control, or who seeks to overstep his bounds. Even as high priest over the people, he fulfills his calling with humility.

> *And behold, when I see many of my brethren truly penitent, and coming to the Lord their God, then is my soul filled with joy; then do* I remember what the Lord has done for me, *yea, even that he hath heard my prayer; yea, then* do I remember his merciful arm which he extended towards me.
>
> *Yea, and* I also remember the captivity of my fathers; *for I surely do know that* the Lord did deliver them out of bondage, *and by this did establish his church; yea, the Lord God, the God of Abraham, the God of Isaac, and the God of Jacob, did deliver them out of bondage.*
>
> *Yea,* I have always remembered the captivity of my fathers; *and that same God who delivered them out of the hands of the Egyptians did deliver them out of bondage.*
>
> *Yea, and that same God did establish his church among them; yea, and that same God hath called me by a holy calling, to preach the word unto this people, and hath given me much success, in the which my joy is full.* (vv. 10–13; emphasis added)

As Alma continues, notice that he does not take responsibility for his success. He gives the glory and honor to God. Alma doesn't need to try to take it for himself, because his self-worth is sure. He knows who he is and understands his relationship to God.

Alma ends his reflections overjoyed at the success of others, having no envy or jealousy. His motives are right. He has no secret ambitions. There is no incongruency—his motivation matches his actions. He has no false façade. He is genuine and authentic.

But I do not joy in my own success alone, but my joy is more full because of the success of my brethren, who have been up to the land of Nephi.

Behold, they have labored exceedingly, and have brought forth much fruit; and how great shall be their reward!

Now, when I think of the success of these my brethren my soul is carried away, even to the separation of it from the body, as it were, so great is my joy.

And now may God grant unto these, my brethren, that they may sit down in the kingdom of God; yea, and also all those who are the fruit of their labors that they may go no more out, but that they may praise him forever. And may God grant that it may be done according to my words, even as I have spoken. Amen. (vv. 14–17)

In order to overcome codependency, we need forgiveness and healing. The power that offers both is the Atonement of Jesus Christ. Go forward and offer your whole heart to God. It may be frightening at first, but doesn't He ask us to experiment on His word? He will be there. He loves us and intimately understands why we do what we do. He knows where we need to go, what we need to experience and learn, and how to overcome all things. This path is what He wants us to walk. It is nothing less than the path to Gethsemane. As Elder M. Russell Ballard declared: "Because our goal is to become more like our Savior and to eventually qualify to live with our Heavenly Father, each of us needs to experience the mighty change in our hearts described by the prophet Alma in the Book of Mormon (see Alma 5:14). Our love for our Father in Heaven and the Lord Jesus Christ needs to be reflected in our daily choices and actions. They have promised peace, joy, and happiness to those who keep Their commandments" (Ballard 2010).

CHAPTER 9

CONTROL AND SAFETY

In order to overcome and destroy the destructive patterns of codependency, we need to go on an inner journey. For that to occur, a basic shift needs to occur for the wounded adult. For most codependents, life exists in the external world. Safety, acceptance, validation, self-worth, power, control—all exist outside of the wounded adult. We look to others to give us self-esteem. We lie, manipulate, and sometimes intimidate others to remain safe and protected. In this environment, the individual yearns to be loved and held and assured that everything is okay.

Many times, the codependent individual will reach out to others in order to prove how much others need the individual. In addition, the codependent person offers help and support, makes great sacrifices, and gives incessantly. He or she tries to save and fix others, often overextending himself or herself, only to end up feeling emotionally and physically exhausted.

Operating from this place is called having an external locus of control, or an external power base. "I am always at the mercy of others—how they see me, how they treat me, what they think of me. I am either trying to influence them to see me a certain way, or I am pushing them away to maintain my safety."

Being connected to the inner person does not come easily. Sins, doubt, darkness, self-hatred, and the artifacts of past trauma—memories and sensations—live within the body, the individual's internal world. Yet that is exactly where we need to go for this change to occur.

The following chart explores the spiritual impact of basing one's power internally versus externally. Notice that when a person's power center is external, he or she is more harsh, more rigid, more afraid.

WHEN MY POWER CENTER IS EXTERNAL—OUTSIDE OF ME	WHEN MY POWER CENTER IS INTERNAL—WITHIN ME
Live according to the letter of the law.	Focus on the higher law, the spirit of the law.
Look outside of me for validation of worth.	My worth exists independent of my behavior.
Safety comes from controlling others.	Safety comes from inside of me, using boundaries.
Strangers' perceptions of me matter most.	God's perception of me matters most.
Public self-image is most important.	Who I am doesn't change—in private or public.
Motivated, driven by sense of shame and perceived rejection.	Motivated by love and compassion.
Always afraid, feeling threatened.	Sense of calm, solid confidence.

As you review the following list of what internal and external forms of creating safety look like, remember that gaining safety is a progressive and ever-adaptive goal. When inner safety techniques no longer work at keeping him or her feeling safe, the individual turns to the outside world and tries to find safety outside of himself or herself.

Internally Based Forms of Creating Safety (Disconnect and run away from self)

Blocking
Stuffing
Numbing
Denying
Rationalizing
Blanking out or zoning out
Normalizing traumatic events
Future tripping—trying to control future
   outcomes or consequences
Becoming overly analytical
Divorcing from my emotions
Compartmentalizing
Creating a fantasy world to escape from
   reality

Externally Based Forms of Creating Safety (Connect with people in wounded ways)

Superficial, creating façades or masks
Intense, engulfing, overwhelming
Emotionally detached
Intimidating
Manipulating, lying, telling half truths
Secretive, creating intrigue, seductive
Controlling, overbearing, dramatic
Always happy and smiling
Never gets angry; passive-aggressive
Making power plays
Saving and fixing others, regardless of what
   they want, "for their own good."
Full of advice
Pious, self-righteous, judging

POWER

The concept of power can be divided into two categories—personal (internal) and interpersonal (external). Personal or internal power involves our ability to think, to feel, and to choose how we will react to situations and people. The ability to choose and have control over our internal life is the hallmark of personal power.

Interpersonal or external power is always limited. Everything that happens outside of an individual's internal world is the realm of external or interpersonal power. In this arena, a person has limited power in terms of what he or she can do to be safe, limited power in terms of influencing someone else, and limited power to change the external environment.

Let's take the experience of being abused and plug in our definitions of power. When a person is abused, his or her ability to stop the experience is limited (external realm). The ability to protect oneself during the event is limited (external realm). The ability to influence the abuser is limited (external realm). During the abuse, the victim does indeed experience a sense of not having enough power to stop the abuse from happening. This promotes a sense of powerlessness. *Powerlessness always exists in the interpersonal or external realm.* How the person feels about the abuse and how he or she chooses to deal with it is within the internal realm, where the individual always has power.

What creates problems is when the person confuses the two realms. A wounded individual wants desperately to gain control and therefore stop the wounding from occurring. Because the victim cannot gain control, he or she sees himself as being powerless. This is personalized, and the victim's internal world is now defined as being unable to stop the abuse from happening. "I am powerless. Who I am as a person is defined by my inability to stop the abuse." So the victim's internal world, where he or she *does* have absolute power, is defined and regulated by the external world. Thoughts and feelings about the abuse are seen as overwhelming and bigger than the person's ability to process and handle them.

The person now sees power as existing outside of himself or herself. The more the individual can control the outside world, the more powerful he or she feels. When thoughts and feelings come up that remind him or her of being powerless, the person finds ways to escape from his or her internal world. The more perfect the escape, the more powerful the person feels.

Tian Dayton explains how trauma can push a person to be externally focused: "When we get scared, our left brain (where language resides) shuts down. What remains very active, however, is the emotional scanning system in our right brain . . . Children who experience relationship trauma . . . become more in touch with what those around them are feeling than what they are feeling. They become habitually outer-focused and may lose touch with what is going on inside of them" (Dayton 2007, 151).

An example of attempting to be safe by controlling others (a sign of trying to gain power externally) is offered by Brenda Schaeffer, an expert in the field of love addiction. She created a list of power plays (see Schaeffer 1986). By doing these behaviors, the codependent is seeking reassurance that he or she is in control. Doing these power plays makes the person feel powerful (even if it is only an illusion) and therefore in control—and therefore safe.

- Giving advice, but having difficulty taking it
- Giving orders; demanding and expecting too much from the other person
- Trying to "get even" with or diminish the self-esteem or power of the other person
- Tending to be judgmental; putting down others to sabotage their success
- Fault-finding, persecuting, punishing
- "Holding out" on the other, not willing to give the other what he or she wants or needs
- Making and then breaking promises; seducing to gain trust
- Making decisions for the other person
- Discounting the other's ability to problem-solve
- Patronizing and condescending—setting self up in a superior role to the other person
- Using intimidation, bullying, bribing, threatening
- Having self-righteous anger, being bitter, holding grudges
- Physical and/or verbal or emotional abuse

When a sense of powerlessness becomes integrated into a person's core concept of who he or she is, then love, esteem, and experiencing one's self-worth become conditional, based on whether or not the individual feels powerless or powerful. Powerlessness is rarely seen as a positive trait.

For codependents, powerlessness is almost always linked to believing that something bad is about to happen, and that they are not safe. And when this idea occurs, they react from a flight, fight, or freeze response. In all cases, these moments of powerlessness occur within interactions the codependent has with other people. The person is not usually aware of his or her extreme reaction, and doesn't see the behavior and thoughts as a problem. It is usually the other person that is to "blame" for the codependent person's actions.

Personal power is as constant as one's worth and value. It is unchanging and infinite. How can this be? Because within us, we will always have the ability to choose how we deal with emotions, thoughts, and experiences. We can't change others, but we can change ourselves. I can't make someone else use the Atonement. I can, however, humble myself and come unto Christ with a broken heart and a contrite spirit. I have the power to surrender my will, my way, my desires, to God.

In order to move from living outside of ourselves (externally driven) to living inside of ourselves (internally focused), we have to turn our will and our lives (how we keep ourselves safe) over to Heavenly Father. The following chart illustrations this idea:

SELF-WILL-BASED FORMS OF PROTECTION	HEAVEN-BASED FORMS OF PROTECTION
REQUIREMENTS • Need to be controlling • Have to be closed, hardhearted • Use defenses and coping skills • Always vigilant, on guard	REQUIREMENTS • Need to let go, trust in God • Be open, humble • Exhibit a willingness to follow • Surrender my will
CORE IDEALS • Fear-based, reactive • Seek for immediate gratification • Right now! • Seek to escape reality • Remove the threat	CORE IDEALS • Faith-based, proactive • Seek for patience • Faith proceeds the miracle • Seek acceptance • Threat not always taken away. Instead God strengthens me, comforts me.
PHYSICAL SENSATION • Numbness, euphoria, adrenaline and altered states • Seek an absence of pain, fear, sadness • Seek intensity and thrills, achieve calm by disconnecting • Cold, empty	PHYSICAL SENSATION • Calm that comforts, anchors, reassures • A solidness, a peace, a quietness, feeling centered • Feeling connected, present, aware • Feeling of warmth, sense of being loved, soothed, nurtured, validated
BEHAVIORS • Deflect and reject reality • Dominate or be passive • Codependent, people pleasing • Use addictions	BEHAVIORS • I go to my knees and pray • Share thoughts and emotions • Turn to the Lord • Wait and be patient

Safety and peace are what we all want, regardless of where we came from or what our childhood experiences were like. Fear is a universal emotion. And because fear does not feel good, everyone tries to overcome it. But true safety and lasting peace do not come from us. We are imperfect, mortal, fallen individuals. Safety and peace can only be achieved by coming unto Christ. Jeffrey R. Holland of the Quorum of the Twelve Apostles stated: "May I be bold enough to suggest that it is impossible for anyone who really knows God to doubt His willingness to receive us with open arms in a divine embrace if we will but 'come unto Him.' There certainly can and will be plenty of external difficulties in life; nevertheless, the soul that comes unto Christ dwells within a personal fortress, a veritable palace of perfect peace. 'Whoso hearkeneth unto me,' Jehovah says, 'shall dwell safely, and shall be quiet from fear of evil' (Prov. 1:33)" (Holland 2003, 66).

PART 3

UNDERSTANDING THE FRAMEWORK

No pain that we suffer, no trial that we experience is wasted. It ministers to our education, to the development of such qualities as patience, faith, fortitude and humility. All that we suffer and all that we endure, especially when we endure it patiently, builds up our characters, purifies our hearts, expands our souls, and makes us more tender and charitable, more worthy to be called the children of God . . . and it is through sorrow and suffering, toil and tribulation, that we gain the education that we come here to acquire and which will make us more like our Father and Mother in heaven.

Orson F. Whitney (Whitney 2012, 98)

Chapter 10

The Codependent Template

By the time a wounded child becomes an adult, he or she does a myriad of behaviors without much thought. Over the years, patterns of behavior are woven into the daily fabric of our lives. Certain thought processes have been used so much that they appear almost automatic. Recovering codependents often say they can't see their behavior until after they've acted codependently. "How can I see something—pick something out—that permeates my every waking moment?" asked one person. "It's like telling a fish to stop breathing water!"

The key is awareness. And yes, in the beginning, our greatest teacher is often the mistakes we make (looking at things in hindsight). With time, persistence, and Heavenly Father's help, we will receive understanding that can help us break free of our codependency. One tool that facilitates that kind of awareness is to learn about some basic patterns of behavior. Only then, when we have something to look for, can we plan an intervention.

A Universal Template

A template is a pattern, burned into the brain, usually due to some intense experience. A template in the brain is just like a template in a computer—if I turn on the machine, it will react the same way, bringing up the same image every time. Why? Because it follows a set pattern— the behavior or choice is already made for the computer. So it is for a person. We act and react according to various templates, set patterns that seem to close off all choices but one. Wounded adults operate from various templates, making it look as if their behaviors are automatic or reflexive. Overcoming past wounds helps the person break the templates and restore choice to the system. The following diagram describes a common template for codependents:

SITUATION (THE UNKNOWN)

FEAR

CONTROL THE FEAR
(My Coping Skills)

When I get triggered (go to my coping skills), there is no need for faith, there is no need to trust God, and my heart becomes hardened.

- Triggers are like a knee-jerk reaction (a seemingly automatic response) that activates old patterns and behaviors.
- These triggers are held in the fragmented, compartmentalized, dysfunctional parts of me.
- Triggers don't originate from the healthy, authentic, functional self.
- I can't make the different choice of turning to God to help me manage and handle life until I see the trigger and understand it.

RESULT

- Freeze, blank out, run away, avoid
- Fight back, be passive-aggressive
- Create power struggles
- Addictions, compulsive behaviors
- Anxiety, despair, giving up
- Deny feelings

Stephen Wolinski, founder of Quantum Psychology, believes that when these "ghosts and demons" of the past pop up in the present day, the wounded adult is slipping into a trance. "Children will create . . . trance states that are most helpful in buffering them against the first experience they are not able to integrate i.e., trauma . . . Since these trance states worked so well in its original context (being abused) the child then uses it to create an automatic response to the environment in general. The environment is no longer experienced as it is in the present moment, but rather as it was in the past" (Wolinski 1991, 20).

John Money was one of the first authors who talked about why we choose the people we choose to date, fall in love with, and form intimate relationships with. He stated that everyone has a "love map" or relationship template that is imprinted on the mind and that helps the person to find his or her "love" (Money 1986, 13–27). In the ideal world, the person's love map would reflect a host of healthy ideas, concepts, and traits that would end in two people coming together and forming a healthy, balanced relationship. However, these love maps can be, as Money puts it, "vandalized" by abuse (ibid 121–35). Suddenly, the person's map can be twisted and distorted, and the template becomes one of dysfunction and future heartache. As another expert puts it, "If our pain occurred in the context of our primary close childhood relationships, the most likely place that our post-traumatic stress reactions will surface is in our primary close relationships in adulthood" (Dayton 2007, 73).

Steps to Creating a Filter

Original Experience

Emotional, sexual, or physical abuse. Lack of bonding or attachment to primary caregivers.

Creation of a Filter

In order to protect the body, a filter is created—like radar. The body is on the lookout for future abuse or future signs of rejection and abandonment. The body assigns meaning to the feelings and sensations felt during abusive incidents, and to feel them again means that one is going to be abused again. It profiles and is on alert for anything that reminds the body of past hurt, pain, or trauma.

Trigger Enacted

As current input passes through the filter, which is based in the past, the body wants to escape from and protect itself from potential harm. Replaying the past (the filter reminding us of the past) as a way to overcome and manage the trigger (emotion or situation that is happening right now) keeps the person locked in a repeating pattern. Based on what the filter is, when the person acts from that perspective, he or she will do certain behaviors. And those behaviors will expend the heightened energy and diffuse the alert. For a moment, we will believe we are in control, powerful, and safe.

Tammy, a Latter-day Saint recovering addict, worked with me to try to discover the specific template or pattern that kept her struggling in her codependency. With time, we were able to identify a major pattern that had been at work for most of her life. She wanted to share what she discovered in case it could help others. Here is her pattern:

How Far I Will Go to Avoid Abandonment

Part 1. The other person makes me feel special, needed, and different (this is what I want to believe). Or I prove to the other person that I am special, different, loyal, helpful, and long-suffering. The other person is always more important than I am. His or her happiness is more important than mine.

Part 2. The other person begins to abuse my trust, abuse me, take advantage of me. The person will drop clues and give hints that he or she is selfish and dangerous.

Part 3. I have to deny all of this to manage the pain of being used, which realization would be devastating.

Part 4. Big explosions happen in the relationship, shattering the fantasy, the dream, the denial. I can no longer turn a blind eye to the other person's abuse—even if I want to.

Part 5. I've finally had enough of being used and abused. I get angry and push the other person away.

Part 6. I become lonely. I can't take it. I reach out and take that person back. I try harder, give more. This time will be different—I'll make sure of it.

This pattern promoted certain distorted definitions for Tammy. The filter through which she saw and interpreted life became faulty. Some of these distorted definitions included:

- Surrendering means to lose control.
- Being lonely means to lose control.
- Becoming genuine (without a mask or façade) is terrifying.
- Authentic love is suspicious. It can't be trusted and must be rejected.

These filters kept Tammy repeating this pattern. Until the filters changed—until her vision was restored so she could see truth—she could not properly use her agency or receive God's help. Dallin H. Oaks of the Quorum of the Twelve explained that "Each of us has a personal lens through which we view the world. Our lens gives its special tint to all we see. It can suppress some features and emphasize others. . . . What we *see* around us depends on what we *seek* in life" (Oaks 1985; emphasis in original).

Clearly, the more spiritually whole we become, the more our filters change. Our filters are no longer twisted or narrowly focused on possible threats. Now our filters are focused on seeing truth, finding beauty and compassion, and looking for the tender mercies of the Lord. What we seek changes. We are no longer looking to fulfill past childhood yearnings, for as we come unto Christ, those yearnings are met and our souls are filled with love and serenity. We seek to receive and offer love from a Christlike place—a place called charity.

CHAPTER 11

AGGRESSOR, VICTIM, AND MARTYR TEMPLATES

What are some other templates seen with individuals who struggle with codependency? There are three types of common templates: identifying with the aggressor, identifying with the victim, and becoming the martyr.

IDENTIFYING WITH THE AGGRESSOR

Why would a person choose to identify with his or her abuser? The most prevalent reason is to try to reclaim lost power. When someone is sexually, physically, or emotionally abused, there is always an unbalance of power, or at least the appearance of a power differential. The person being victimized will feel helpless and powerless over the situation. It becomes very easy to believe that the abuser is all-powerful, even godlike.

No one enjoys feeling helpless and powerless. Many wounded adults had little in terms of support and guidance when they were children. In the absence of someone to offer an example of exhibiting and using power for good, these children looked to their *only* example—their offender. And there is nothing more powerful than to "feel" the energy, force, and sheer will that is exhibited by the offender while he or she is abusing you.

Satan will encourage and magnify the belief that to feel powerful or be powerful, one must do what the offender did. The implied promise is that the abused person will never be the victim again. That is the basic theme for this template. If the offender is the parent, this template becomes second nature for the child. It is a difficult thing to hear, but one that is true. All wounded people, on some level, at some time, will identify with those that have hurt them and exhibit some type of aggressive or offending behavior.

A person who identifies with the aggressor exhibits these types of behaviors and attributes:

- I meet my needs at the expense of others.
- I often blame, lie, justify, and minimize to avoid getting in trouble.
- I am often controlling in a relationship, either as the rigid person ("It's my way or the highway) or the person who will bend over backwards for you ("You can't live without me").
- I lash out with my anger.
- I lie to make things go my way.
- I stare other people down with my eyes.
- I routinely invade other people's personal space.
- I am often arrogant and cocky.
- I use my position at work to make things go my way.
- I use my voice—yelling, screaming, swearing—to cause others to back down.
- I create dependent relationships with others. I need people to need me.
- I have trouble admitting or even seeing my faults.
- I find myself attracted to broken people. In these relationships I am the "fixer" or "savior."

IDENTIFYING WITH THE VICTIM

Whereas the aggressor template uses manipulation, seduction, intrigue, grooming behavior (creating a false sense of trust with someone to promote one's own agenda), and sometimes even coercion and intimidation to achieve its goal—that of safety first, and "love" second—the victim template operates in a much different manner.

It may sound strange at first, but there are just as many ways to get connected and meet one's needs by being the victim as there are by being the aggressor. This hit home to me one day when Andrew, my second son (six years old at the time), came to me with a bird in his hand. He said he noticed it flopping around in the back yard. Apparently its wing was broken. Andrew got a shoebox, put a bunch of toilet paper in it, put the bird in the box, and held the box reverently. My wife called the Humane Society, and they directed us to a veterinary clinic that took in injured wild animals for free. Andrew and I drove there and dropped off the bird.

As we gave the box to the vet, there were tears in my son's eyes. "Is he gonna be okay?" he asked fervently. The vet assured him everything would be all right. As we drove home, there was a sense of satisfaction on the little boy's face.

So what happened to the bird? It got the care it needed by advertising—whether it wanted to or not—that its wing was broken. Luckily it was a sensitive six-year-old boy who saw and heard this, instead of a hungry cat. With adults who have been hurt by abuse, it is no different. Instead of embodying the godlike stance of their aggressor, some remain stuck as victims.

Sometimes they saw a parent they identified with being routinely beaten. Sometimes they saw no abuse at all, but modeled their behavior after a parent who had unresolved abuse issues of his or her own. Vogel explains that mothers who have unresolved abuse issues are likely to promote victim behaviors and victim mentality within their children, even if the child has not been abused (Vogel 1994).

The victim template goes something like this: "If I act wounded, defenseless, broken, dependent, and helpless, someone will come and take care of my needs. I will receive love, nurturing, comfort, and protection."

Another "benefit" of acting this way in a relationship is that the person never has to take responsibility for anything. He or she never has to grow up and find his or her functional adult self. And for every "wounded bird" that uses the victim template, there is someone out there looking to be a savior.

Spiritually, being a victim means I will forever wait for Jesus to find me, open the door, and carry me across the threshold into His peace. But what does the Savior say? We must search Him out. We must knock. We must ask. (See 3 Nephi 14:7–11.) Even if our attempts are puny and weak, we must at least make the attempt.

The adversary promotes the idea that our mistakes, sins, and weaknesses are not our fault. We can blame others for our unhappiness. We look outside of ourselves for solutions. Satan extols the virtues of remaining a helpless child or victim. If he can get us to abdicate our agency and give it to someone or something else, he wins.

A person who identifies with the victim exhibits the following types of behaviors and attitudes:

- I am overcritical of myself. "It's always my fault."
- I take responsibility for everything bad that happens.
- My worth and value is based on what I can give to you.

- I am a *yes* person. I please others. Then they will like me and meet my needs (even though I often don't tell other people what my needs are).
- I beat myself up for making mistakes—I will punish myself endlessly instead of moving on. I get stuck in my mistakes.
- I think too much.
- I worry and obsess too much. Usually I do this with situations that are beyond my control, or are unsolvable in the short term.
- I let my partner decide where to go for dinner, or what movies to see. I rarely care. When my partner asks what I want to do, I almost always return the question—"Well, what do *you* want to do?"
- I say yes to situations where I want to say no.
- I have my partner pay the bills and balance the checkbook. I almost never know how much money we have. I ask my partner if it's okay to buy something for myself.
- I'm afraid of conflict. For example, if I order a meal and it comes wrong, I usually eat it anyway without saying anything.
- I am sick a lot—with headaches, body pain, and other nondescript symptoms.
- I have trouble being alone.
- I get easily overwhelmed by daily living.
- I will change my values and lifestyle when I am with someone I love or want to love.
- I find myself attracted to others who are headstrong. Even if I think the person is different than the other jerks I've dated, most of my girlfriends or boyfriends end up putting me down, acting aggressively, and sometimes even hurting me physically.

BECOMING THE MARTYR

A major concept in the victim template is the martyr/victim "dance"—the two sides to the coin of being a victim. Like so many other attributes related to codependency, being a martyr is often seen as a good or noble thing. To see how this behavior becomes twisted, let's start off with defining the term *martyr*. A martyr is to be someone who makes great sacrifices or experiences great suffering for a cause or a belief. Joseph Smith was a true martyr. Joan of Arc was a martyr. The women and children that were thrown into a pit of fire for believing the gospel taught by Alma and Amulek (see Alma 14) were martyrs. Countless Saints in all ages were martyrs.

However, in the upside-down, counterfeit world of codependency, being a martyr has no noble or endearing qualities. We might say or think, "I did this for you, and I don't even get a thank you?" or "After all the love and sacrifice, this is how you treat me?" or "Fine! I'll just keep on being unappreciated—no, no, you just stay put while I serve you."

Sarcasm, hostility, and resentment, with a heavy helping of guilt trips and shaming tactics, become tools of the codependent martyr. "On the surface, the self-sacrificing martyr sounds sincere when he or she encourages you to go ahead with your plans and not to worry about anything. But if you fall for this, you'll regret it later when the martyr's real feelings emerge with the resulting anger, resentment, bitterness, and negativity" (Wasson 2006). Why? Because nobody is giving the wounded adult what he or she wants—to be seen, to be hoisted up on others' shoulders and heralded as a person of infinite worth.

Charles Shahar explains: "On a deeper level, martyrs are very needy for love. Unfortunately, they unconsciously believe that the only way they can get love is through suffering. The suffering makes them feel special and wanted, and it brings meaning to their life. Their suffering is tied to their ego. They are actually proud of it. Take away their suffering and they seem lost" (Shahar 2006). Within this framework, the definition of a martyr looks quite different.

MAKING GREAT SACRIFICES,
EXPERIENCING GREAT
SUFFERING . . .

FOR A CAUSE OR A BELIEF

This is how I will achieve my goals. My suffering, denying myself so I can be there for you, so you can then be there for me, is worth every ounce of blood, sweat, and tears. Every sacrifice, in the end is for me.

The "cause" is to take care of myself, to create safety and control, to be my own "savior," to do it my way. Survival is always selfish. I must put me first. "I WILL be seen. I WILL be loved. I WILL be safe. I WILL be taken care of—you WILL not ignore, discount, reject, or abandon me.

When the desired goals or outcomes are not met, the person flips the coin and retaliates from the place of enraged victim. The thinking goes something like this: "You have hurt me, spurned me, and now I am justified in fighting back. I will reject the rejecter. I don't have to take responsibility for any of my actions because you didn't accept me, love me enough, or give me my due. You didn't make me feel special or important."

The victim will pout, throw a temper tantrum, slam doors, be dramatic, or fall into a heap on the floor and cry. One way or another, the codependent will try to get his or her needs met. Maybe, just maybe, the other person will feel sorry for not reacting the right way and give the wounded adult what he or she yearns for—validation.

Being a martyr encourages the person to do service, to give and be selfless, but to need others to see the good works he or she has done. The sighs, the sacrifices, the long stories of how much the person worked to make a dinner or a project or a fireside go off well are all geared toward enticing a response. "Oh, Sister Brown, you do so much for us," or "Brother Jones, we couldn't have done it without you."

And when the praise is given, what do martyrs do? Push it away, discount it, minimize it. Later, they will mutter under their breath how nobody acknowledges the great sacrifices they are making, how they are the only ones who do anything in the ward. As martyrs serve, their resentment and bitterness builds. The martyr is akin to the publican or the Pharisee of the New Testament—two-faced, hypocritical, wanting to take the glory for himself, making sure everyone knows of his suffering and sacrifices.

Examples of a martyr mindset include:

- I am extremely sensitive to any type of constructive criticism.
- I will lament and sigh at my heavy burdens, but when someone offers to help me, I get angry at the person and/or won't allow him or her to help.
- I often perceive constructive criticism as a personal attack.
- I see many interactions during the day as unfair. I seek for fairness, but when I am asked to hold to the standard I expect from others, I demand that an exception be made.
- I make others aware of how they have wounded me (which often exceeds a normal reaction to the same event) through sarcasm, veiled "get-backs" under the guise of humor, or pouting.
- I struggle with low self-esteem and often deny my self-worth.
- I want and need constant validation from others that I am worthy of love, admiration, and affection. This often makes others become tired of me and not

want to be around me. I can then use that as an indicator that how I see myself (as unwanted and unlovable) is accurate.

- If I do something nice for you, I will routinely bring it up. I can't let you forget it.
- I will sacrifice my needs and wants for others. I will then remind people how much I am sacrificing for them.
- I have been told I use guilt trips on others and that I nag a lot. I don't see it, though.
- I struggle with being passive-aggressive.

Identifying with the aggressor, identifying with the victim, and identifying with the martyr are templates that wounded adults often use in relationships and within themselves. The templates used in the individual's relationships are the same ones he or she uses with himself or herself.

Adults with unresolved childhood wounds are notorious for beating themselves up, denying themselves compassion or forgiveness, and generally acting and judging themselves harshly. They also are known to regularly run from responsibility, deny themselves opportunity for healing, and ruminate in self-pity.

These templates must be destroyed, reworked, and replaced with new, healthier templates. How will that happen? We must heal the old templates, let them grow old and unused. The only way to do that is to create and use a new template—one that is spiritual in nature. We will explore this spiritual template later in the book. For now, just remember that God always prepares a way out. Following Him never gets us stuck, trapped, or chained down. He is the Author and Creator of peace, freedom, and hope.

Chapter 12
Magical Qualities

One major stumbling block in overcoming codependency is that of assigning magical qualities to others. We whitewash someone's imperfections and weaknesses. It becomes very easy to idealize him or her, and up goes the pedestal. At least partly, we idealize someone so we can believe we see in him or her the traits we want to see in ourselves. For a child, idealizing the parents is akin to creating a Higher Power—God—out of them. The parents are infallible. Trust is built upon the belief that the parents really can do what the child believes Mommy and Daddy should be able to do. They should *always* be there. They will *never* let you down. They will *always* respond to your needs with love and concern and kindness.

For a child, this is a normal part of development. Children naturally see their parents as all-knowing, all-wise, all-protecting. With time, the healthy, functional goal is that the children will move beyond this stage. Yet many codependents remain stuck—frozen—in this developmental stage. The person is still looking for "the other" to soothe the fears of that little boy or girl inside. So idealizing someone, putting him or her on a pedestal, making that person your "God"—all these behaviors come from the wounded individual's unfinished sense of self.

Jane talked about her first sponsor. Her experience is a good example of assigning magical qualities to someone else. The following comes from a journal assignment she allowed me to use.

She was very spiritual, and I wanted so much to be like her. And then the day came when she told the group she had slipped and returned to her bottom-line behavior a few nights before. I was crushed. Here was this woman that I thought was perfect. Of course she wasn't—I was simply seeing the humanness of my sponsor. I didn't want to accept the fact that this woman was human and frail like me because I only wanted to open up to someone and be vulnerable with someone whom I could trust one hundred percent to never let me down. I was still in that childlike, immature place. I wanted to place all of me in her "capable" hands.

Assigning magical qualities to someone leads to idealizing that person, and the codependent individual ends up creating a suitcase full of expectations about how that person should or should not behave. When an individual lives according to his or her expectations about a partner, it is a sure-fire way to find disappointment and excuses for returning to maladaptive behaviors.

Here's another example from Jane. Her first sponsor had moved, and she was looking for another one. A woman started coming to group that reminded Jane of her first sponsor. She asked the woman if they could get together. As Jane was driving to their meeting place, she created the expectation that they would quickly connect and get down to the business of working through some recovery-oriented workbook. She quickly learned that this woman's agenda was very different. The woman simply wanted to talk, take it slow, and then decide if they were compatible. Jane got very angry. She called this woman selfish and self-centered in her head. Then Jane started to feel sad. She thought she would never find someone to work with and would always be alone. She became depressed and got even more angry at this woman for not wanting to work with her. All this drama because Jane went to the meeting with expectations.

Expectations are our hopes of how we want things to be, how we want reality to change to suit our needs and desires. Some examples of expectations are:

- When I come home from work, I expect dinner to be ready and the kids to be calm and relaxed.
- I expect to become a leader in the ward. I'll be the next Young Women president or the next bishop.
- I expect my children to always make the right choices.
- At school, I expect my friends to always play with me during recess.
- I expect my spouse to meet my sexual needs—every time I ask.
- When I go to the club, I expect that men/women will want to dance with me.
- I expect my parents to meet my needs (even when I'm thirty-two).
- I expect my spouse to understand what I mean when I ask, "Do you want to do something tonight?"

- When I go to my college classes, I expect that no one will notice me.
- I expect that everyone will think I'm fat and unattractive.
- I expect men/women to flirt with me.
- When I go to the job interview, I expect to make a fool out of myself and not get the job.

Larry, a member of an LDS addiction recovery group, put it like this: "Having expectations sets us up for future resentments." Living a life without expectations essentially means that I will not future-trip (live in the future and constantly try to control the future). I will truly be in the moment and accept what is, instead of railing against reality because it is not how I would have it.

Yet living without expectations is graduate work in our healing from codependency. Along the way, I can learn to stop and ask myself what my expectations are for the day, and then express them to my spouse, boyfriend/girlfriend, roommate, or coworker. Making our expectations known decreases arguments, contention, and hurt feelings. If we communicate our expectations, they change. They don't have to be hidden absolutes that will crush us if they are not met. The other person can give feedback and correct erroneous hopes or goals, and we can come to agree on shared expectations.

In a general Relief Society meeting, President Dieter F. Uchtdorf spoke about idealizing others and living with unrealistic expectations. He said: "God is also fully aware that the people you think are perfect are not. And yet we spend so much time and energy comparing ourselves to others—usually comparing our weaknesses to their strengths. This drives us to create expectations for ourselves that are impossible to meet. As a result, we never celebrate our good efforts because they seem to be less than what someone else does" (Uchtdorf 2011).

Heavenly Father has hopes for all of His children. He tells us what needs to happen for us to return to Him again, and then lets us decide what we want. He communicates—is always communicating—with us. Nothing is hidden, hinted at, or secretive. He speaks clearly and openly, and he never speaks out of both sides of His mouth. He will remain a loving and kind God regardless of what we choose to do. We can throw a temper tantrum because our spouse didn't do the dishes (even though we didn't ask him or her to—it was a secret expectation), but God will never change His course, His behaviors, or His attitudes based on our behavior. He may lament our choices, He may feel sad, but He will never turn His back on us.

Communicate your thoughts and feelings. Let others know where you are coming from. Realize you cannot always control the outcome so it will be in your favor. Allow yourself to see others in the light of day. Don't minimize your spouse's drinking. Don't rationalize away your spouse's compulsive overeating. Don't deny what your spouse is doing on the internet. Sit with reality and then to turn to God and say, "I see this. This is what I think about what I'm seeing. And this is what I'm feeling about it. Please help me. This is bigger than me." And He will be there, speaking comfort to your heart and giving direction to your mind.

Chapter 13

Fear of Abandonment

Codependency, like most maladaptive patterns of coping, exists on a continuum. In the middle are general forms of codependency, some of which are very common behaviors. At either end of the continuum are more extreme forms of the disorder. It looks something like this:

EXTREME CODEPENDENCY: AVOIDANT BEHAVIORS	GENERAL FORMS OF CODEPENDENCY	EXTREME CODEPENDENCY: OBSESSIVE BEHAVIORS
Fear of intimacy	Fixer, caretaker	Fear of abandonment Do all/be all Needless and wantless People pleaser

Sometimes, based on past histories, a person will operate in the extremes, rarely hitting the middle. For others, living in the middle of this continuum over time can magnify and push the behaviors to become more and more extreme. And there are always those that move from one extreme, going all the way through the codependent continuum to the other extreme. In other words, the codependency continuum shows that the more extreme the codependency is, the more extreme the behaviors will be. No matter how it plays out, however, there is no healthy place to be on this continuum.

The following chart offers deeper insight and meaning into how a person can live in the extremes. Take time to study it and see if you find yourself in this pattern.

LOVE AVOIDANCE/AVOIDANT
"I will make you leave me."
Create space in relationship.
Push others away, feel suffocated with closeness.
"I'm going to keep you at arms' length."

LOVE OBSESSED/ANXIOUS
"I will make you love me."
Create dependence: "I will make you need me."
Keep hanging on no matter what. "Don't leave me."
No sense of self without the other person.

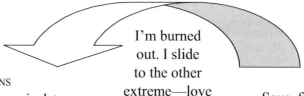

I'm burned out. I slide to the other extreme—love avoidance.

ACTIONS
Hide out, withdraw, isolate, or act compulsively. Keep busy, get lost in a project. Argue, knit-pick, being impatient.

EFFECT
Promote self-pity, self-hatred. No intimacy. Feel lonely. Desire to be nurtured, soothed, comforted.

FEARS
Being used. Feeling pain, sadness, grief. Being rejected. "Being loved is scary, even though I desperately want it.

To live in either state, I end up re-creating or reliving the past trauma in the present. I am trapped by the past—reacting to past messages, past fears, past threats. This leaves me in a wounded state. Change remains elusive.

I can't stay in this state indefinitely. It gets too lonely. I find myself sliding to the other extreme—love-obsessed and anxious.

ACTIONS
Save, fix, rescue, help, people please, always extending resources, always say yes. Always "on." Very busy. Prone to be passive. Doesn't confront issues.

EFFECT
Emotional exhaustion. Burned out, depressed, feel heavy and overwhelmed. No intimacy. Secret resentments. Judging, jealous.

FEARS
Afraid of being abandoned, rejected, forgotten. I do not want to be left out. I do not want to be seen as "less than," no good, worthless, or undesirable. I'm afraid my need for love can never be quenched.

Let's review each end, starting with the obsessive behaviors (fear of abandonment) extreme form of codependency. At this end of the continuum, beliefs become more twisted and distorted. Actions become obsessive. Fear of being abandoned increases dramatically. Obsessive thoughts, feelings, and behaviors seep into daily life. Relationships become things to control, to grab onto like a drowning victim being thrown a life preserver. The following are signs of being in an obsessed-with-my-partner-and-afraid-of-being-abandoned relationship:

- A feeling of powerlessness around the other person
- A lack of control in the relationship
- Acting passive due to fear of the other person leaving
- An obsessive preoccupation towards the other person (where you can't stop thinking about him or her). Can lead to stalking.
- Breaking up and getting back together multiple times
- A compulsive urge to be with the other person more and more
- Discounting one's own feelings in order to "keep" the other person—discounting one's anger, fear, etc
- Recurring thoughts of losing one's partner—fear of him or her leaving the relationship for someone else.
- Attempts to "win" over one's object of affection, using money, gifts, etc
- Keeps coming back for more, regardless of how he or she is treated

Newman and Berkowitz state that "an adult, when he loves, does not risk his whole identity. That he already has, and will have however the other responds. If he loses his lover, he will still have himself. But if you look to someone else to establish your identity for you in some way, losing that person can make you really feel destroyed" (Newman and Berkowitz 1986, 74). The relationship-obsessed codependent needs his or her partner—husband or wife—to validate the codependent's sense of worth. The codependent person's identity appears to spring from the relationship. It is as if he or she is a blank canvas outside a relationship. His or her sense of self is created and supported by being in the relationship.

One of the main characteristics of extreme codependency is that the codependent is attracted to someone who cannot offer love. Therefore, the codependent will attempt many different behaviors aimed at finding, securing, and keeping the object of his or her affection. This leads to the codependent person controlling the partner. The more a codependent believes he or she is in control and has power over his or her partner, the safer the codependent will feel, and the more secure he or she believes the partner's love is.

Furthermore, in many cases the codependent has not even fully matured into a functional adult. For example, a twenty-five-year-old woman may still be a frightened eight-year-old girl on the inside. Having an adult relationship with a child does not work. The common theme is that the relationship-obsessed codependent is viewing love from a child role.

Neediness, pity, being rescued, being the rescuer, and even attraction are all components of childhood. A child is needy and dependent on others. A child craves compassion and empathy as he or she makes a lot of mistakes. A child is naturally in the role of needing to be rescued. A child likes to feel powerful and will try to imitate the parental rescuer role in play and same-age relationships. And a child is easily infatuated with people, whether it's the kindergarten teacher, a grandparent the child doesn't see very often, or a gentle and kind neighbor.

From this immature, broken, fragmented, and twisted place, love becomes more about control and less about real love. In this state, love becomes synonymous with self-soothing and meeting one's needs. There is no charity here. There is no self-sacrifice, respect, or compassion for the partner, unless it will get the codependent what he or she craves—safety and protection (power and control).

The following list of traits of immature, codependent love is adapted from Brenda Schaeffer's work (see Schaeffer 2009).

- Feels all consuming
- No sense of self outside of relationship
- Fears letting go
- Fears risk of change
- Allows for little individual growth
- Lacks true intimacy
- Plays games
- Gives to get something back
- Attempts to change partner
- Needs partner to feel complete
- Demands unconditional love
- Looks only to partner for self-worth and affirmation

- Fears abandonment upon routine separation
- Attempts to take care of partner's feelings
- Plays power games—"one-upmanship"

Someone who is still acting from an emotionally wounded state is operating from the past and can't be in the present. Relationships formed in these settings make it next to impossible to remain in the present. Even more difficult is that most extreme codependents are already in an existing relationship—unable to separate from their parents. With the past unresolved, the bonds formed by trauma keep the person trapped in this relationship, impacting present-day interactions.

Many codependents are single and feel deep pain, fear, and anxiety about being alone. Being able to face themselves and address their core issues before pursuing a relationship is crucial for many reasons. It takes time for a relationship-obsessed codependent to see and identify his or her pattern of creating intrigue, connection, engagement, enmeshment, and intensity.

Also, especially during the beginning of health and healing, a codependent will start to feel emotions—to see reality—and this will be uncomfortable. Even if it doesn't seem like it, with all the good intentions and rationalizations, most boyfriend/girlfriend relationships formed while an individual is new in recovery are about escaping from this new (and often painful) connection with oneself.

Taking a back seat to the object of his or her affection, the extreme codependent becomes needless and wantless due to fear of losing his or her partner if demands are made of that partner. This type of codependent puts all of the blame, guilt, and responsibility of the relationship onto himself or herself and constantly tries harder and harder to please the partner as a way to "keep" him or her.

The signs that a codependent is receiving or will soon receive his or her much-needed sense of security and validation become the reinforcers for the obsessive behaviors. These behaviors include convincing someone that he or she needs the codependent, ensuring that the codependent's partner won't leave, and working desperately to make his or her fantasy about the partner become a reality. Every little sign, indication, or clue that the other person is bending to the will and desire of the obsessed individual motivates him or her to continue that course of behavior. The person the obsessed codependent latches onto becomes his or her God, his or her "heroin," his or her everything.

Extreme codependents will fear abandonment, or exhibit what Brennan calls "rejection anxiety" (Brennan et al. 1998). During therapy, one obsessed codependent described what it was like to live in this state of constant fear and anxiety about being abandoned:

Fear ruled my life. It became such a constant, I actually stopped recognizing the emotion. It became the norm—not the exception. As I became healthier in my recovery, I could see how fear had affected almost every aspect of my life. I was afraid of being betrayed, being rejected, feeling pain and shame, being alone, and being hurt and used by others. I was afraid others would find out the secret—that I was essentially unlovable, worthless, not enough, and defective.

Unfortunately, most codependents only know how to create relationships where they either end up pushing others away (causing abandonment), or where they attempt to connect and be intimate by getting lost in their partners (whereby emotional intimacy is never fully formed). In the end, the very thing the codependent fears most is what he or she actually re-creates over and over again. Tanni, a Latter-day Saint recovering codependent, put it this way, "When we use our coping skills, we get exactly what we were afraid of getting in the first place."

I asked Bill to write about how he acted in his obsessive, extremely codependent state. He and I had been working together for a few months, and he was starting to get a real awareness of his behaviors and patterns. These are his words.

I'd fall "in love" completely and hopelessly on the first date—sometimes even before that. I'd lose my personality and become whatever my partner wanted me to be. I could only feel good about myself if I had someone in my life. It didn't matter if it was a boy or a girl. The summer I was twelve, I baled hay for a neighbor. The farmer's nephew had come to stay with them for the summer and we clicked right away. He and I became fast friends. I couldn't wait to see him each morning. If he was coming over after work, sometimes I'd race outside to wait for him. I felt exhilarated when I was with him, like I was alive. I was so sad and lost when he went home at the end of the summer. This happened over and over with different people.

As time went on, it progressed. I became emotionally attached to other women even after I was married. It was like having sex with someone's feelings. We'd share our fears and dreams, and form this intense connection—not really intimacy, but it sure was a pretty good counterfeit. I often thought I loved these women, and if they ever gave the signal, I'd leave everything to be with them. Eventually the relationships would fade away. It wasn't thrilling or exciting anymore—no more electricity. This was my definition of nurturing—the crackle of excitement as I saw the other person walking towards me.

It didn't matter if the women were my supervisors, cab drivers, neighbors, coworkers, or even check-out girls at the local grocery store. There were no such things as boundaries or ethics in my life. There was one rule that took precedence over all others—to make people love me, want me, need me. And to that person, I'd give all of me. What was really crazy was that I never saw what I was doing. There was no awareness of the big picture—no thought of others, never any consideration of the future consequences. I just needed to satiate my craving to be "loved."

So, what can be done? What is the prescription for overcoming this debilitating condition? While it may seem self-centered to some, the primary relationships that recovering individuals need to focus on in the initial stages of recovery are the relationships they have with themselves and God.

Until a person can form a proper relationship with his or her inner self and begin to understand who he or she is, there is little to give to a partner. Wounded adults have spent many years lost in the haze and fog of obsessive, compulsive, codependent behaviors and are lost even to themselves.

A recovering codependent cannot be fully present and intimate in a relationship until he or she has worked at becoming reunited with God and begun healing through the power of the Atonement of Jesus Christ. Hidden, self-deceptive motivations, ingrained patterns of behaviors, and distorted beliefs cannot be overcome without the help of our Heavenly Father. By being born again spiritually, the recovering individual becomes honest and aware of himself or herself, and others. Relationships are now based on spiritual principles rather than on self-protective, survival ideologies.

Chapter 14

Fear of Intimacy

In the last chapter, we reviewed the form of codependency that involves extreme obsessive behavior based on fear of abandonment. But many codependents actually *avoid* love, becoming restless around persons who might provide genuine care and nurturing. In these cases, the closer the wounded adult comes to obtaining love, the more he or she pushes away a partner or potential partner. This move, becoming avoidant and trying to create emotional distance within the relationship, is fueled by a fear of intimacy.

A codependent person using avoidant behaviors tends to:

- Have trouble saying no
- Lack the energy to maintain intimacy
- See desire for intimacy as a sign of neediness
- Fear being engulfed and overwhelmed by his or her partner
- Feel guilt and shame for being unable to remain in a relationship
- Withdraw from social interactions
- See himself or herself as trapped by loneliness
- Stay aloof when interacting with others, or become very charming and outgoing
- Become exhausted in the presence of others, even if he or she likes them
- Experience panic as intimacy evolves
- Feel disconnected from grief and have trouble recognizing loss
- Be a workaholic as a way to avoid relationships
- Have parents who were overly involved or controlling in his or her life

- Withdraw from his or her partner when stressed
- Have experienced some form of abuse

The above list was influenced by Pia Mellody's ideas on love addiction and love avoidance (see Mellody 2003).

Most avoidant individuals experienced enmeshment in their childhood or youth, and this is a major reason they fear intimacy. Let me take a moment to explain what the term *enmeshment* means. The prefix *en* means to put or get into. *Mesh* is to knit together, or anything that entangles, snares, or traps. The suffix *ment* means the state, condition, fact, or degree of being. Therefore, *enmeshment* is the state of being entangled and trapped in a relationship, with the other person "knit" into us.

In such a relationship, boundaries are blurred or nonexistent. It becomes difficult to know where you as a person end and the other person begins. Emotions appear to be easily transferred between enmeshed individuals. Beliefs and values of one partner appear to be taken on by the other person. One becomes a spokesperson for the other. Instead of two distinct people, enmeshed individuals become one—in thought, word, emotions, and actions.

The typical avoidant has had an enmeshed relationship with at least one of his or her parents. While such an intense relationship can have rewarding moments (feeling special, getting special treatment, being on the inside—knowing more than other siblings), it is also suffocating and scary for a small child to be so lost inside another person. As an avoidant enters into a relationship, he or she enjoys the euphoria of the newness of the relationship. As intimacy begins to occur, however, the avoidant will feel suffocated and trapped. He or she will do things to try to create space within the relationship or even end it.

The other problem with being in an enmeshed relationship with a parent is that the child has difficulty breaking free of the parent, and as the child grows into adulthood, he or she has difficulty finding a sense of self. The adult will ask questions like, who am I? What do I like? What do I want to do with my life? This is because he or she has been "lost" or trapped inside the enmeshed parent.

Someone who has been sexually abused can also experience the sensation of being trapped and suffocated. In this scenario, sexual abuse creates a physical as well as emotional sense of enmeshment. The child is still being used to meet the adult's needs. The child can feel powerless and engulfed by the abuser. The abuser can frame the abuse as a sign of love, sometimes calling their child victim a boyfriend or girlfriend. The child often picks up ideas from the abuser about who the child is, what he or she is good at or good for, etc. The victim of sexual abuse often has the same reaction as someone who has experienced emotional enmeshment.

The problem is that the avoidant's definition of love is to become enmeshed with the other person. Therefore, every time the avoidant tries to find love, he or she will end up running from it. This makes for a lonely existence. From this place of enmeshment, distorted ideas are formed about love and intimacy.

Myths about Receiving Love

Here are a few myths about receiving love:

- If I open up to love, I will be engulfed and suffocated.
- If I open myself to love, I will become dependent—a victim—and defenseless.
- If I open myself to love, I will experience terrible pain and sadness.

Myths about Giving Love

The following are myths about giving love:

- If I give love, I will be rejected.
- If I give love, I will be seen as needy.
- If I give love, I will never be able to give enough.

The struggle for the avoidant is that he or she, like everyone else, wants to feel love and closeness. Regardless of emotional, physical, and/or sexual wounds from the past, there is still an intrinsic desire for the security, affection, and healing that comes from love. In a relationship, the avoidant will often come in fast and make intense connections. As the relationship continues, the avoidant will start to distance himself or herself from his or her partner. If the relationship continues, eventually the avoidant person will seek to re-ignite the passion and intensity that used to be felt in the past. With time, distancing will occur again.

Most avoidants are very good at beginning relationships, but horrible at keeping and maintaining them. Avoidants will pull in their love interests, but once the connection happens and the relationships becomes deeper, they push their partners away. Some codependents push away love as a test to see if their partners will continue to love them even when they are acting disagreeable or unpleasant. This behavior is a result of the conditional and irregular love the wounded adults experienced as children from their caregivers. So, the avoidant codependent remains alone, tortured by fear of the very thing he or she wants—love, security, affection, and nurturing.

As the avoidant sees the relationship he or she is building with another, and as intimacy begins, withdrawal will occur. The person will withdraw physically or emotionally or both. Codependent avoidants can be men or women. They struggle to maintain friendships—same sex or otherwise. Once in a relationship, an avoidant will often feel overwhelmed, suffocated, and emotionally exhausted.

In order to create space within a relationship, an avoidant codependent will do the following. See if any of these fit with what you do in a relationship.

- Cause arguments
- Stay up after partner has gone to bed
- Become obsessed with work or some other activity
- Be defensive, turning arguments back on the other person so he or she seems at fault
- Avoid calling a friend back
- Avoid parties
- Create a life on the computer (chat rooms, internet games), choosing that life over interactions with "real" people
- Compulsively flirt with other people
- Avoid physical affection (snuggling, holding hands, etc.)
- Act flamboyant and charming outside of the relationship, and withdrawn and sullen inside the relationship
- Feel a sense of shame about who he or she is, allowing guilt and shame to be motivating factors for what he or she does in a relationship

There are some avoidants who never seek out people. They struggle to be around others and are often reclusive. They may want relationships and are sick and tired of being so lonely, but see that first step as too much. Many suffer from depression. They can go months and years without being in a relationship.

Avoidant codependents often go from A to Z in a relationship, skipping all the other letters of the alphabet in between. Therefore, they easily mistake attraction, intensity, and lust as love. The more intensely connected the individual is to a partner, the more he or she believes he or she "loves" that partner—and vice versa.

Physical and sexual attraction is often mistaken as love. The thrill of attraction is often what binds and connects an avoidant with someone else. The energy that flows between two new lovers is the best imitation of intimacy for the avoidant.

As day-to-day routines set in, life becomes dull and boring for the wounded adult. Therefore, whenever a relationship deepens, the avoidant "falls" out of love with his or her partner and starts to think about leaving or having an affair, or at the very least, creating space in the relationship. The avoidant is always searching for the "love of my life" that will light up the night sky forever. This level of intensity never lasts forever, so the avoidant searches for that elusive love that will never be.

Ultimately, avoidance is all about being safe. Often, the codependent who acts out in an avoidant manner has a high need to protect himself or herself from feeling deep sadness, fear, and shame. Like an addict, an avoidant often deals with emotions by ignoring them, blocking them out, and disconnecting with them, when it comes to his or her primary partner.

On the other hand, obsessive codependents seek to become enmeshed with their partners. The closer the codependent can get to the other person, the safer he or she feels. Having been so deprived of bonding and emotional attachment to one or both parents, the obsessed codependent yearns for someone to embrace him and her and never let go.

Avoidance is about withdrawing emotionally from oneself and others. Essentially, it is an addictive measure to try to protect oneself from experiencing intimacy. The end result is that the avoidant is terribly lonely. Sometimes it is hard to understand this apparent contradiction of fearing intimacy yet continuing to pursue it. In the end, both extreme forms of codependency have a hole that needs to be filled. Being alone sooner or later puts the codependent way too close to those wounds—those little children screaming to be taken care of, nurtured, affirmed, and loved. Therefore, running after intimacy momentarily feels good and is a distraction.

While intimacy is almost always experienced as intensity for an extreme codependent, as long as that concentrated and passionate energy exists, all is okay with the world. It is when that shadow counterfeit disappears and reality starts to set in that the fear returns. So, the wounded adult runs away from the fear, ends up alone, runs away from being alone, gets in a relationship, ends up hating or fearing the reality as the fantasy vanishes, runs away to escape the budding intimacy, and on and on.

Just as with other, more obviously unhealthy behaviors, codependent people who use avoidant behaviors are trying to protect themselves by being in control. Often the control comes through acting in a compulsively sexual manner, or acting very flamboyant sexually, or being constantly seductive and flirtatious. Some avoidants try to remain inconspicuous (as they may have done as children to avoid abusive attention) but still be the ones making the decisions in their primary relationships. They remain behind the scenes, pulling the strings. They also reject before they can be rejected. Sometimes this is out of fear that they will be hurt first; they reject their partners as a sort of preemptive strike. Other times, the fear is the opposite—that things *will* work out, that the love offered is real. The avoidant person has no idea what to do in this unfamiliar situation, so he or she panics and rejects.

CHAPTER 15

ATTACHMENT

One of the most fundamental lessons we learn in life is how to create and maintain a relationship. John Bowlby, the father of attachment theory, stated that there is "no variable that has as far-reaching effects on personality development [as] a child's experiences within the family. . . . There is a direct link between childhood attachment patterns, adult attachment styles, and functioning in intimate and romantic relationships. Early childhood patterns are unknowingly recreated in our adult relationships" (Bowlby 1983, 369). Whom we turn to and the type of relationship we form is typically a reflection of the attachment we had as infants and children.

Colin Ross explains that attachment will happen—there is no question or choice in the matter. "There is a deep blood bond that is built into your DNA and brainstem—just like the migration behavior of birds" (Ross 2002, 12). However, what happens when it is not safe to attach to the primary caregiver? According to Ross: "The result is a profoundly divided sense of self, and disorganized, ambivalent attachment patterns that fit the disorganized behavior of the parents. In the end, the world must remain split in order to avoid really knowing and feeling the basic reality of childhood: I love the people who hurt me and I was hurt by the people I loved" (ibid 16).

TRAUMA AND ATTACHMENT

All forms of abuse will affect the child's ability to attach to others in some way. Why? Because "we're literally wired to experience love, warmth, and a sense of well-being through closeness and to fear abandonment" (Dayton 2007, xv). Not getting these variables causes us to react in maladaptive ways. *We end up having to rewire ourselves for survival, not for closeness and intimacy.* Trauma disrupts, halts, or freezes developmental processes. Abused children must designate resources to survival that would normally be devoted to their growth and development. This reallocation of developmental resources, coupled with a lack of nurture and support from the child's primary caregiver, places the child at risk for poorer development and an inability to regulate his or her emotional and physical states (Punamäki 2002). Dayton writes, "Children who want to preserve their connection with their parents above all else will likely come up with whatever strategy they need to insure that bond. These child solutions can stay with us throughout life if they are never reexamined, especially if they get frozen into place by fear" (Dayton 2007, 7).

The closer in relationship the offender is to the child, the more disruptive the attachment will be. Emotional neglect has been found to be more damaging to attachment relationships than either physical neglect or other forms of maltreatment, with the exception of sexual abuse. In general, three-quarters of all those who struggle with PTSD have attachment problems. (Muller et al. 2000.)

While reviewing their past as they work on their codependency, many people explain that they did not experience abuse. However, when it comes to bonding, people do not have to experience abuse to have their attachment weakened. Apart from the stressor of not being able to connect with their primary caregivers, many children with maladaptive forms of attachment have depressed parents. To a child, a depressed parent is seen as inaccessible and unresponsive (Porter 2003). A parent's mental health issues—depression, anxiety, bipolar disorder, etc.—can indeed have an impact on bonding and forming secure, healthy attachments with their children.

A child with attachment problems, if the problems are not treated or corrected, usually grows into an adult with attachment issues. The type of attachment experienced by a child "continues to influence behavior, thought, and feeling in adulthood" (Fraley and Bonanno 2004). Most often, the problem the parent had in attaching successfully with the child becomes the very behavior exhibited by the child as he or she grows into adulthood.

An adult with attachment problems will exhibit the following types of behavior:

- *Impulsiveness.* Indulging in impulsive behavior that is often regretted later.
- *Negative and provocative behavior.* Exhibiting a negative mindset that causes the individual to deliberately excite or annoy others.

- *Desire for control.* Exhibiting a strong desire to control surroundings and manipulate people and events. The individual may use means like lying and cheating, and even stealing, to do so.
- *Resistance to love and guidance.* Struggling to connect, empathize, or sympathize with anyone. The individual also faces difficulty in giving and receiving love and affection from others. He or she has trouble developing feelings of closeness, and struggles to allow others to nurture him or her.
- *Lack of trust.* Failing to develop trusting relationships with others. Generally speaking, a person with attachment disorder does not trust anyone.
- *Anger and agitation.* Feeling depressed, deeply sad, and isolated. The individual is overcome by stress and frustration. However, he or she conceals these traits by showing anger. The person may do this by means of destructive, cruel, and hostile behavior, and may often argue with those who don't agree with him or her.
- *Superficial positive traits.* Appearing very charming. Such an individual can easily engage others in long and interesting conversations.
- *Addictions.* Indulging in substance abuse such as alcohol and drug addiction. The person may also suffer from an addiction to gambling, or even to work.
- *Helplessness.* Feeling unable to help oneself to connect or bond with another person. This is due to the symptoms of isolation and depression.
- *Lack of responsibility.* Refusing to take any responsibility for one's negative actions. The individual is unable to handle conflict with others.
- *Confusion.* Feeling confused, puzzled, and obsessed with finding answers to his or her questions. This confusion leads to the individual's general lack of concentration, and a disability to direct his or her attention toward any activity for long.

CHAPTER 16

CONDITIONAL LOVE

A wound that often occurs in childhood is that of receiving conditional love, where the child believes he or she must do something in order to gain a parent's love. Of course a child must be held accountable for his or her actions, but when expressing, giving, and/or showing love to a child is tied to his or her behavior, wounding will occur. When the parent acts in an abusive manner and does not take responsibility for his or her actions, he or she is implicitly teaching the child that the abusive act is the child's fault. If Daddy never owns his anger, it must be someone else's fault. If Mommy never apologizes for yelling, she must be justified in losing control.

Having a parent that doesn't take responsibility for his or her behaviors, or that blames others for his or her feelings and reactions, or has unrealistic expectations for his or her children, is causing wounds in those children. Why? Because a child cannot manage what the parent is asking him or her to handle—not biologically, not emotionally, and definitely not spiritually. Dayton offers the following concepts to support this idea.

- "Our ability to feel comes before our ability to think, which is why children aren't in a position to make sense of what they're feeling when they're small" (Dayton 2007, 46).
- "The child is completely dependent on his or her parent to act as an external regulator because his or her own internal regulators won't be fully developed until around age 12 . . . That is why the small child is so vulnerable to emotional and psychological damage when the home is chaotic" (ibid 5).

The parent that appears disconnected, aloof, or overly busy and then is suddenly engaging and showering the child with affection is an example of a parent giving conditional love. The parent that berates the child when he or she makes mistakes, but does not applaud the daily good choices the child makes, is another example of conditional love. The parent that has extreme, unreachable expectations for his or her child promotes conditional love. The child that is physically abused will come to believe that love is based on whether or not he or she can keep Daddy or Mommy from getting angry. That is conditional love. The parent that spotlights the child that is doing well and compares that child to his or her other siblings (or neglects the other siblings) is showing conditional love. Truly, there are countless ways a child comes to believe that love is conditional.

The following list shows the thought process, attitudes, and beliefs a child forms when experiencing conditional love:

- My works equal my worth.
- My usefulness equals my worth.
- My success or failure is based on others' choices—how you respond to what I do.
- I internalize everything—if I don't feel love from Mom or Dad, it's my fault.
- I am a people pleaser.
- I adopt others' rules and expectations, meeting them in order to gain acceptance.
- If I don't do something right or perfectly, there is not just an absence of love, but outright rejection (I spill the milk and my parent rages; I try to mow the lawn and get yelled at for not doing it right, etc).
- If I don't measure up, I beat myself up (punish myself), deny myself happiness, and/or sabotage my success. At least then I am in control of whether or not I will get love.
- I isolate from God, from His love and comfort.
- I reject all goodness that could come to me.
- I let my mouth go and don't filter what I say, to force rejection from others. They are going to reject me and not love me anyway.
- I deserve to be alone.
- I deserve abuse and pain.
- I do not deserve good things. I will make sure I don't succeed.

Satan uses this twisted foundation of conditional love and whispers to us: "It's good for you to be there for others. It's *not* okay to reach out when *you* need help. That is a shameful thing to do, and you should feel guilty." You ask, "Why?" The adversary replies, "Because your worth and value depend on you being 'good enough' to handle problems by yourself. You have to be strong, figure this out, and be good, honorable, and righteous. Your power comes from being very independent—standing against everything by yourself. After all, your power, worth, and value are fluid variables. They can be taken or lost very easily. Surrendering, letting go of your will, just shows how weak, stupid, and worthless you are. Stop being a baby—man up!"

Christ, on the other hand, refutes these ideas. We are not alone. We do not have to do everything by ourselves. He counsels us to always remember Him (see 3 Nephi 18) so He can heal us (see 3 Nephi 9). He will teach us all things we should do, starting from the smallest and most basic skills. He will teach us like He taught Nephi, revealing step by step how to build a boat, even though Nephi had never done anything like it before.

This new way of living, with new skills and new beliefs and a new perspective, only comes as we humble ourselves like little children (see Mosiah 3:19). We become more dependent on Christ, not less. We surrender and turn to Him. And He will take care of us and protect us.

When we attempt to overcome past wounds, we will eventually come to see that the journey is about ourselves and the Lord—not our parents, other family members, or our abusers. Overcoming the past is not about placing blame or pointing fingers. Remaining in a state of bitterness, resentment, and blame towards parents and/or abusers impedes the individual from achieving a sense of codependent sobriety and maintaining change. Forgiveness of our sins and transgressions and feeling peace cannot come until we let go of that hatred and bitterness. Staying in the victim mode keeps us from feeling the effects of Christ's Atonement.

The pain inflicted on us may have been given to us by another, but we must deal with it. Only we can take our painful wounds to the Savior. In doing so, we take responsibility for ourselves and come to feel comfortable with that responsibility.

CHAPTER 17

CARRYING MY PARENTS' BAGGAGE

Abuse occurs when a parent has trouble with boundaries and violates or disregards his or her child's boundaries. When the parent or primary caregiver acts in such a manner, a part of him or her is disowned. For example, the parent who yells at his or her son or daughter for failing a test is disowning his or her own feelings of shame or fear—shame for yelling and scaring the child, and fear brought on by the poor grade. Who will pick up that discarded, orphaned emotion? The child will.

Is this a real phenomenon? The answer is a resounding yes. We are built to connect—emotionally, spiritually, and biologically. Heavenly Father designed our bodies to help us achieve certain goals and objectives. The body, an important part of the soul, helps the spirit learn, grow, and become more than what it could be by itself. The following quote by Dayton underscores this reality:

> *Our nervous systems are constructed to be captured by the nervous systems of others, so that we can experience others as if from within their skin. . . . We have the apparatus necessary to tune in to another person, literally built into our own biology through the mind/body phenomenon of mirror neurons. Mirror neurons track the emotional flow, movement, and even intentions of the person we are with, and replicate this sensed state by stirring in our brain the same areas active in the other person. . . . Our nervous systems are not self-contained, but inter-dependent; they connect with those of the people close to us in a silent, holding rhythm that helps regulate our physiology. The nervous system of all humans—and for that matter, all mammals—are interconnected.* (Dayton 2007, 25–26, 28)

When a parent hides, disowns, or stuffs emotions, energy is given off. Vulnerable individuals—usually children—end up picking up or "carrying" that displaced feeling. And the resultant impact on that child can be severe. In many cases, maladaptive coping behaviors (addictions and codependency) originate from carried beliefs or emotions.

An example comes from one addict's experience with his father when he was a child. He went to see his grandparents and was going to stay with them for a week. The boy was very excited. Suddenly his father raged at him in front of his grandparents. His father was acting shamelessly and didn't own the emotion. If the father had, it would have stopped him from acting abusively. But he didn't, and the boy picked up all the energy of that experience. He carried his father's shame and took it on as if it were his own. This kind of scenario happened repeatedly. His own life was filled with shame, yet much of it wasn't his. His self-esteem suffered. He sabotaged success because he didn't think he was worthy of it. He was always apologizing and putting himself down.

A woman I worked with had a strong sense of self-hatred that fueled some pretty devastating compulsive behaviors. No amount of therapy seemed to dislodge it. Then she told me about how her mother had been love-crazed and obsessed about her cheating husband (my client's father). Her mother became suicidal during the pregnancy and even tried to kill herself. On some level, this client continued to carry throughout her life this message from her mother—"I'm not worthy of love. If I can't get someone to love me, I deserve to die. I don't deserve to live."

When she and I worked on these messages and gave them back to her mother, a dramatic shift occurred in this woman's life. The next week when she came back, she was beaming. "I'm free!" she exclaimed happily. I asked her what she thought had happened.

"It wasn't me that wanted to die—it was Mom. Somehow that idea got inside of me and I owned it. But once I let it go and realized that wasn't my belief but my mom's, this huge burden was lifted. I felt full of light, like this dark shadow had disappeared."

Here's another example. Gina was deeply embarrassed about making money and spent it compulsively. As soon as she got it, she had to spend it. She routinely racked up credit-card debt and was on the verge of declaring bankruptcy for the second time when she came to see me. As we explored her family's history with money, she was able to piece together that her money issues were not hers but her father's. Gina was carrying her father's intense hatred towards his parents, who were very wealthy but never showed him any love. His parents were obsessed with making money and often shipped him off to relatives or left him alone while they worked long hours at the office. His wound of being abandoned and being less important than money surfaced in the form of hating money. Even though Gina's father rarely spoke about his parents and never talked about money (to the point that Gina noticed it), she picked up all that unspoken anger and energy emanating from her father.

One last example. Sarah was raised by an invalid mother and a verbally abusive and intimidating alcoholic father. Her mother died when Sarah was ten years old. Sarah sat at her bedside and often nursed her. She tried to help her mother, but on some unspoken level, Sarah knew she could not save her. Her mother would moan and talk about her regrets. She felt so powerless to protect her children from their father—powerless about so many things. Sarah's mother was a true victim. Toward the end of her life, Sarah's mother would often cough and choke, gagging on her own blood.

Years went by. When Sarah married and had children of her own, she developed intense neck pain. Her children had difficulties, and Sarah often felt powerless to fix them. When her second son became a serious addict, she exhausted all of her resources trying to save him. For seven years she fought to tear him away from his drugs. All the while, her neck pain became so bad it often forced her to stay in bed for days at a time.

Sarah came to see me to help her disconnect from her son. She eventually told me of her mother's death. Strikingly, Sarah described her mother's choking as though she was being strangled. And that was what Sarah's neck pain felt like—like she was being strangled. As she was able to finally mourn her mother's death fifty years later, and let go of all the regrets her own mother had unknowingly put on Sarah (as well as her victim mentality), Sarah's neck pain became more and more manageable. It subsided to the point that when she feels it now, it is seen as a sign that she is not addressing an issue and needs to stop what she's doing and check in with herself.

Without boundaries, parents throw out unspoken messages—disowned emotions—and the child is often the one to pick them up. Unfortunately, when the child picks up the disowned energy from his or her parents, the child usually ends up owning the belief or emotion as if it was his or her own. Like a sponge, the child soaks up everything said and not said and internalizes it. Without boundaries, parents end up promoting unhealthy and destructive patterns of behavior in their children.

Even though he does not have a body, Satan has learned how to distort, hijack, and twist human development. He knows how a body works. He has studied it and knows its many weaknesses. He understands psychology very well, and he knows how important emotions are. He perverts emotions, through sin and darkness, to create stumbling blocks for us.

As we have already discussed, abuse, sin, and our parents' baggage become perfect vehicles for Satan to trick us and confuse us as we pick up and carry others' feelings. Whenever I sin, I will push disowned emotions and energy onto someone. When that happens, whether I am aware of it or not, I become a servant of the devil, sowing seeds of future problems, stumbling blocks, and sin in that person. Whether I know it or not, I have helped the adversary plant a veritable garden of sadness, misery, despair, and discouragement in the other person's life.

Satan wants us to feel overwhelmed and hopeless, because then he can destroy trust and love and make it easier to give up the fight. He wants us to feel alone and abandoned—like nobody is there for us or cares about us. Again, in this state, it is easier to get us to fall to temptation.

The adversary will create counterfeits to authentic emotions. He will lead us to believe that lust is really love, that intensity is really intimacy, and that a rush or surge of excitement, stimulation, and heady sensations is what the Spirit feels like.

Emotions help foster and create intimate connections with ourselves, others and God. They inform us and help us be safe. They help us to achieve balance with our intellect. They help us to treat others with respect. It is only by using our emotions and being in touch with them that we can follow Christ's admonitions:

> *Therefore all things whatsoever ye would that men should do to you, do ye even so to them.* (Matthew 7:12)
>
> *And the second is like unto it, Thou shalt love thy neighbour as thyself.* (Matthew 22:39)
>
> *The Lord God hath given a commandment that all men should have charity, which charity is love. And except they should have charity they were nothing.* (2 Nephi 26:30)

Heavenly Father, through the Holy Ghost, will help us regulate our emotions. Authentic emotions, experienced within someone who has good boundaries, never take us to sin and darkness. True emotions—expressed emotions—are often the vehicle through which God speaks to us, comforts us, and guides us. The following chart reflects the gifts we receive from our emotions and the impact these feelings can have on our behavior.

EMOTION	GIFT	BEHAVIOR
Anger	Strength, determination	Action
Fear	Caution, prudence, sensitivity	Discretion, dignity, self-preservation
Pain/sadness	Empathy, hope	Respect boundaries of self and others
Joy	Contentment, peace of mind	Celebration, devotion, growth
Passion	Perseverance, commitment	Adherence to personal values
Love	Intimacy, vulnerability, confidence	Compassion, tenderness, openness
Guilt	Motivation for change	Change of behavior
Shame	Humility, accepting our humanity	Surrender, service, tolerance

PART 4

HEALING THE CODEPENDENT HEART AND MIND

*Wherefore, my beloved brethren, if ye have not charity,
ye are nothing, for charity never faileth. Wherefore,
cleave unto charity, which is the greatest of all, for all
things must fail—*

*But charity is the pure love of Christ, and it endureth
forever; and whoso is found possessed of it at the last
day, it shall be well with him.*

*Wherefore, my beloved brethren, pray unto the Father
with all the energy of heart, that ye may be filled with
this love, which he hath bestowed upon all who are true
followers of his Son, Jesus Christ; that ye may become
the sons of God; that when he shall appear we shall be
like him, for we shall see him as he is; that we may have
this hope; that we may be purified even as he is pure.*

Moroni 7:46–48

CHAPTER 18

UNDERSTANDING THE CONCEPT OF RECOVERY

Many people wanting to address their codependency have an unclear vision of how to do so. The word *recovery* is often used to refer to the process of healing from codependency. Most people think of addiction when they hear the word *recovery,* and they dismiss it because they are not addicts. Yet the process of working to overcome codependency is essentially the same as working toward overcoming an addiction.

Recovery means we are improving, finding, and reclaiming who we were created to be. And who were we created to be? We are spiritual beings living in a mortal world, with perfected Heavenly Parents. Truly, we are children of God, trying to become like Him. Therefore, recovery helps re-establish the spirit, not the body, as CEO, the driving force behind choices and decisions. Recovery breaks the knee-jerk responses, the deeply embedded patterns of thought and behavior, and reclaims agency. Passions, fears, and unrestrained emotions will no longer chart our course.

Recovery takes the natural man out of the soul and restores it to its true spiritual form. Now the body and the spirit work together in harmony. Now the body facilitates change, not just maintaining the old status quo. Within the human body are many functions that help not only create change but then anchor that change so it becomes a part of us. Muscle memory is an example of this. How the brain learns and functions also reflects the body's ability to take a new behavior and make it a habit. The brain is created to find shortcuts, so that if we want to do something or react to something badly enough, the brain will create a pathway. Over time, that pathway can actually become a shortcut or a "new" knee-jerk reaction. Yes, the body is a vital tool to help us repent and change.

Recovery changes the filters through which we see and experience life on earth. No longer will distorted beliefs, half truths, and lies be the lens through which we see and interpret life. As our perspective changes, we will come to see our trials and our day-to-day interactions from a spiritual, true, eternal view.

Recovery is overcoming the fallen, dysfunctional ways of living. We realign ourselves with God's way of living. We submit to Him in meekness and humility, allowing the Holy Ghost to guide us. This is part of what being born again refers to—the spirit gaining mastery over the body, the spiritual overcoming the carnal through the Atonement of Jesus Christ.

The prophet Alma told his son Shiblon to "be diligent and temperate in all things . . . not lifted up unto pride; yea, see that ye do not boast in your own wisdom, nor of your much strength. Use boldness, but not overbearance; and also see that ye bridle all your passions, that ye may be filled with love" (Alma 38:10–12). What a perfect synopsis of what is required for codependent recovery.

Claudia Black, an expert in the field of codependent recovery, offers an overview of the journey. She focuses on overcoming emotional and psychological barriers, stumbling blocks that keep us from achieving a new way of living. Indeed, overcoming codependency requires us to address all areas of our lives—emotional, mental/intellectual, physical, and spiritual. The following list is adapted from her book, *Changing Course.*

- Recovery is actively taking responsibility for how you live your life today.
- Recovery is being able to put the past behind you. It is no longer having your childhood script dominate how you live your life today.
- Recovery is the process in which you develop skills you weren't able to learn in your childhood.
- Recovery is no longer living a life based in fear or shame.
- Recovery is developing your sense of self, separate from survival/coping mechanisms. Your identity is no longer based in reaction, but action.
- Recovery is the process of identifying, owning, and developing healthy ways of expressing feelings. It is the process of learning self-love and self-acceptance.

CHAPTER 19

UNDERSTANDING CHARITY

Charity is what codependent sobriety looks like. Charity is the opposite of codependency. Charity comes from a healthy place, and codependency comes from a place of fear and dysfunction. Charity is the answer to the questions, so what do I do? How do I change? What does healthy look like?

In its most simple definition, charity is how Christ loves, and how we should love Him. What motivates His love and what His love looks like are also encompassed in the word *charity*. The Savior's love for us is pure, perfect, and everlasting, much like His atoning sacrifice on our behalf. Indeed, we may say that charity was one of the motivators behind that incredible redemptive act.

Yet, as so often is the case, repetitive words or phrases can lose their meaning. We speak them without connecting to the real connotation of the word. With all the catch phrases and buzz words spoken over the pulpit and in the classroom, *charity* is one word that demands our attention and understanding. Charity is linked to repentance, a new heart, being born again, becoming true followers of Christ, and even to gaining eternal life with the Father.

Charity is essential to salvation. In talking with Jesus Christ, Moroni spoke of charity and how necessary it is to have it: "And again, I remember that thou hast said that thou hast loved the world, even unto the laying down of thy life for the world, that thou mightest take it again to prepare a place for the children of men. And now I know that this love which thou hast had for the children of men is charity; wherefore, except men shall have charity they cannot inherit that place which thou hast prepared in the mansions of thy Father" (Ether 12:33–34).

Gene R. Cook of the First Quorum of the Seventy gave a great discourse on charity during April 2002 general conference. He outlined three suggestions to help us gain charity:

1. Recognize His love. "Pray . . . with all the energy of heart" for this gift . . . It is part of the gift of charity to be able to recognize the Lord's hand and feel His love in all that surrounds us . . ."

2. Receive His love in humility. Be grateful for the gift and especially for the giver of the gift. True gratitude is the ability to humbly see, feel, and even receive love. Gratitude is a form of returning love to God . . . You will come to know He understands your anguish and will, in compassion, always respond to you in love. Receive it. Feel it. . . ."

3. Convey His love. The Lord's response to us is always filled with love. Should not our response to Him be in kind, with real feelings of love? . . Unless you are feeling love, you cannot convey true love to others. (Cook 2002)

Elder Cook goes on: "Some have said charity is love plus sacrifice—a seasoned love. Perhaps charity is to love as faith is to belief. Both faith and charity take action, work, and sacrifice. Charity encompasses His love for us, our love for Him, and Christlike love for others" (ibid).

The great prophet Mormon explained the need to pray for charity. Why is it that prayer is essential in obtaining this priceless gift? Perhaps because charity is a spiritual gift, and as with all gifts from God, we can only receive it as we seek it out. Doctrine and Covenants 46:8 reminds us to "seek ye earnestly the best gifts." In verse 9, the Lord assures us that we don't have to be perfect to receive spiritual gifts: "For verily I say unto you, they are given for the benefit of those who love me and keep all my commandments, and him *that seeketh so to do"* (emphasis added). The gift of charity—celestial love—can only be bestowed on us as we come unto the Savior. Just as we cannot make ourselves be born again, or be the agents of changing our natural state, or overcome the effects of the Fall by ourselves, so too charity comes from God. Our job is to seek it out, search for it, and prepare to receive it.

Mormon goes on to describe the gift of charity: "And charity suffereth long, and is kind, and envieth not, and is not puffed up, seeketh not her own, is not easily provoked, thinketh no evil, and rejoiceth not in iniquity but rejoiceth in the truth, beareth all things, believeth all things, hopeth all things, endureth all things" (Moroni 7:45). This extensive list can seem overwhelming and unachievable. Yet many of the traits Mormon speaks of are variations on the same theme, and point to broader spiritual principles. Look at the following chart:

SPIRITUAL TRAITS	BROADER SPIRITUAL PRINCIPLE
Suffering long Beareth all things Endureth all things	Patience even in the face of pain, suffering, and discomfort.
Believeth all things Hopeth all things Rejoiceth in the truth	Acceptance of reality as it was, is, and will yet become.
Envieth not Is not puffed up Thinketh no evil Rejoiceth not in iniquity	Beware of being judgmental and prideful. Seek humility and a strong sense of self-esteem and self-worth.
Is kind Is not easily provoked Seeketh not her own	Showing a tempered response, exhibiting self-control, and fostering a spirit of outreach and service to others.

Patience. Acceptance. Strong sense of self-worth. Tempered responses, self-control. Developing a spirit of outreach and service. These broader spiritual principles are the ingredients that create, build, foster, and protect love. Being judgmental and prideful, doubting one's worth and value, and unbridled emotions will destroy love. Charity, then, becomes the ultimate, spiritual form of the human emotion called love. Charity is not only the supreme type of love, it is also the greatest way to protect love. Someone with charity will champion love, guard it, and respect it. Without charity, an individual lacks the ability to feel empathy for others and is ruled by his or her own appetites and desires.

Charity it is the form and type of love the Savior feels, expresses, and bestows upon us. Charity is His motivation, the swellings of His heart as He reaches out to us, teaches us, molds us, and helps us to be born again in His image. He offers compassion mixed with firmness. He extends mercy intertwined with clear, forthright direction. He calls people to repentance, shows them their sins and weaknesses, and does so without being malicious or cruel. His one and only motivation is to do the Father's will, which is to bring the Father's sons and daughters home. That singleness of purpose is born from a deep and abiding love for His Father and for us, His spirit brothers and sisters.

And who are we without charity—without Christ's pure love? What state do we operate from before we are able to achieve charity? The natural man. The natural man, as King

Benjamin taught, is the state we live in whenever we go after our own ways, our wills, our base desires (see Mosiah 3:19). Elder Cook declared: "Some destroyers of men's love and peace include but are not limited to: fear, perfectionism, envy, unsubmissiveness, doubt, anger, jealousy, unrighteous control, unbelief, impatience, judging, fostering hurt feelings, pride, contention, murmuring, seeking for honor, competition, lying. All of these are of the natural man, and not of the man of Christ" (ibid).

I pray that when we see Him again, we will be like Him. May our countenances reflect His countenance. May our hearts feel as He feels. May we be born again, taking upon ourselves His ways, His motivations, His thoughts.

The best news? All this is possible. We just need to be willing.

Chapter 20

Accepting Your Worth and Value

The more you become aware of your patterns of codependency, the more you will be able to arrest it. The more you are okay with being you, the healthier your relationships will be. Since a major trait of codependency is defining one's worth and value based on perfection or meeting unrealistic expectations, becoming healthy requires a shift in how you see yourself. You won't beat yourself up anymore. Gone are the self-pity and self-loathing. You will come to treat yourself with love and respect, even when you make a mistake. You will treat yourself and see yourself as God does. The following is a list of behaviors that indicate self-love.

- Being able to acknowledge and praise yourself
- Having confidence in your abilities
- Allowing yourself to feel pleasure without guilt
- Loving your body and seeing its good qualities
- Letting yourself win
- Letting others inside instead of remaining lonely
- Following your intuition
- Taking credit for what you did
- Trusting yourself
- Forgiving yourself
- Letting in affection
- Being responsible for meeting your own needs
- Developing your creativity
- Talking to yourself lovingly and gently

Rory worked with me as his marriage crumbled around him. A little too late, he began to work on himself, hoping it would save the relationship. He came to see how his inabilities to love, to communicate, and to let go of anger, as well as his isolation and his eventual sexual addiction, impacted his marriage. He saw, for the first time, the wounds that offered fertile ground for these "weeds" to grow and infest his family life.

His heart was sincere. He truly wanted to change. He hoped his wife would see the work he was doing, but she had made her decision. As the day of the divorce approached, I asked him how he was doing. He began to cry, explaining that he was really struggling. "The divorce just proves what my dad always told me—that I am a disappointment and a failure and worthless."

To help Rory understand the concept of worth and value, I drew the following diagram on the whiteboard in my office:

THE TRUTH

As Rory and I talked about this little diagram, we were able to distill a thought process composed of five points—ending with a greater understanding of our worth and value.

1. Doug: What your father said to you, how he treated you, says everything about him and nothing about you.

   Rory: But I am afraid. Who am I if I discard the only thing that's been told to me about who and what I am?

2. Rory: Who am I?

   Doug: You are not a perfect person. No one is. In this earthly state, all are fallen, all are hardened (see Alma 34:9). Your behaviors alone cannot ensure your return to Heavenly Father.

   Rory: If I am not perfect, does He stop loving me? Does He stop trying to help me?

   Doug: Did He offer the greatest sacrifice He could offer—allowing His Only Begotten Son to be sacrificed so His children have the chance to return to Him— only to redeem worthless, pathetic, useless pieces of garbage? No.

3. Doug: Therefore, your worth and value cannot be measured by your actions. It must stand to reason that your worth and value exists independent of what you do.

4. Rory: Do the consequences that I experience in this life—good or bad—denote or express my worth and value?

   Doug: Your sins do not make you "less than." Being worthy of going to the temple is not the same as having worth. Remember that Jesus came to publish peace and hope and salvation to the sinners—the sick who needed a physician.

   Rory: But what happens if I get excommunicated?

   Doug: God uses all of His resources to reclaim the lost soul. If excommunication was a sign that the person had lost his or her worth and value, God would do nothing to reclaim that person. The Atonement would not be eternal or all encompassing. But it is, and God does love you no matter what your standing is in the Church.

5. Doug: Your worth and value is a constant; it cannot be decreased. "For behold, this is my work and my glory—to bring to pass the immortality and eternal life of man" (Moses 1:39). This is the measurement of your worth and value—how much God is willing to do, to pay, to sacrifice in order to rescue you.

Rory shed some tears that day, and not just tears of sadness and despair. In fact, by the end of our discussion, he and I both had tears of hope and love streaming down our faces.

Recognizing that he was a personage of infinite worth and value, regardless of the chaos he was working through, gave him hope. This knowledge helped him to discard secret beliefs he'd had about himself for a very long time. And it freed him of many self-destructive patterns, allowing him to repent.

Lowell Bennion, a noted LDS educator, counselor, and author, made the following remarks about the past and God's love:

> *Sometimes we think that God loves us to the extent that we please him, to the extent that we're good boys and girls, good men and women. Love from God is not earned. It is not merited; if it is, it is justice and reciprocity and reward. Love comes from a loving heart, and God's love is unconditional. And he loves the worst of us and the best of us equally, I believe.*
>
> *The past that some of us regret at certain points is not as fixed and rigid as we ordinarily think it is. If you have shameful moments in your past, you're prone to isolate them, to make them rigid, and to think of them as being fixed. You can change your past. You can't change single events in the past, but you can change the past as a whole.* (Bennion 1981)

Chapter 21

Avoidance and Vulnerability

One night during a women's group I facilitate, Tammy, who was introduced in chapter 9 of this book, stated that she hated the word *vulnerable*. It made her physically nauseous whenever someone said it. In looking at this reaction more closely, the group and I came up with the following ideas about vulnerability.

Definition of *Vulnerable* from an Abused, Broken Place

An enemy will attack weak spots, so there is an urgent, life-or-death need to protect and hide our weak spots or weaknesses. Being vulnerable means to offer up those weaknesses to the enemy. There is only one type of outcome when that occurs—pain, suffering, being used and abused, and possibly death. The enemy is potentially anyone. Being vulnerable means to let down all defenses and become totally exposed. This definition and view of vulnerability comes from the adversary. This is Satan's counterfeit explanation. And he uses the sins of others to prove his point—"See, you let down your guard with your mom/dad/neighbor/friend, and you got hurt. It's bad to be vulnerable."

This twisted definition of vulnerability is also supported by the immature, childlike places within us. These little parts of our psyche still see and react as if they are small and powerless. From this place, trying to hide our weaknesses usually creates fear and chaos. There is an element of pride in this survival mechanism. Humility and a penitent heart cannot exist in this "lockdown" state of being. Living according to this meaning of vulnerability only leads to more maladaptive coping skills. There is no healing, no recovery, no change, and no growth from this place. And that is how Satan likes it.

Definition of *Vulnerable* from a Spiritual and Whole Place

From a spiritually centered place, being vulnerable is to be real and honest, sharing our personal reality with others. It is a natural outgrowth of being in a functional, born-again state. A vulnerable person is open, willing, and humble. Being vulnerable essentially means to have a broken heart and a contrite spirit.

A Broken Heart

If your heart is broken, you will:

- Feel emotions
- Be subdued
- Know your defects and shortcomings
- Be humble
- Be real, genuine, authentic
- Be aware of limitations—"I am true to me."
- Communicate from a place of self-honesty
- Trust God
- Be able to experience a personal connection with the Savior's Atonement
- Experience godly sorrow
- Have realistic expectations for self and others
- Have the ability to sit in the present moment—to feel, to meditate, to be aware

A Contrite Spirit

If your spirit is contrite, you will:

- Be teachable
- Be malleable, moldable (one definition of *contrite* is to be ground to pieces or worn out)
- Be willing to admit wrongdoing
- Listen, trying to understand another's point of view or experience (have empathy)
- Be willing to change
- Be curious, open to discovery

- Realize it's all right to not know everything
- Be willing to see your wounds—own your history, your life story

Only from this place can healing occur. Being vulnerable with the Lord is essential if you want to receive the blessings outlined in Ether 12:27: "And if men come unto me I will show unto them their weakness. I give unto men weakness that they may be humble; and my grace is sufficient for all men that humble themselves before me; for if they humble themselves before me, and have faith in me, then will I make weak things become strong unto them."

You cannot have humility without experiencing vulnerability. You cannot experience connection with God without exhibiting vulnerability. You cannot have your weaknesses turned to strengths without becoming vulnerable. Codependency cannot be overcome without becoming vulnerable with the Lord.

Vulnerability does not mean you let go of self-protection. Vulnerability is not about becoming exposed. Rather, it is a state of being where intimacy can be experienced. And true intimacy only happens when boundaries are intact. True intimacy means you are aware of who you are and can share that with someone else. Sharing yourself does not and indeed cannot happen unless you remain connected to yourself. That means you can only share himself or yourself with someone else if you have good, strong boundaries. And boundaries are a form of protection.

Heavenly Father wants you to have good, strong boundaries. Doesn't He tell us to put on His armor? Doesn't He want us to stand strong, firm, and immovable when the enemy attacks? The answer is a resounding yes. "Put on the whole armour of God, that ye may be able to stand against the wiles of the devil. For we wrestle not against flesh and blood, but against principalities, against powers, against the rulers of the darkness of this world, against spiritual wickedness in high places. Wherefore take unto you the whole armour of God, that ye may be able to withstand in the evil day, and having done all, to stand" (Ephesians 6:11–13).

CHAPTER 22

BOUNDARIES AND WILLFULNESS

Author's Note: This chapter comes from the journal of Tanni, a recovering codependent who is a member of the LDS Church. She hopes the insight she received will be helpful to others.

One day Doug and I were working through how to help my kids deal with each other better—how to decrease the contention, the get-backs, the "it's not fair" statements—when he brought up the idea of boundaries. As we talked about what boundaries are and what happens when we don't have them or have broken boundaries, the Spirit offered insight and direction to our discussion. It was a miraculous session. Doug asked me to write down what we talked about so that the ideas would get inside better and help me to "own" them.

Boundaries help us to stay physically, emotionally, and spiritually safe. Boundaries support respect and love. Having boundaries is essential if we want to access the Atonement of Jesus Christ. Why? Because without boundaries, we don't care about others. We don't respect others. We act mean and cruel and selfish. Without boundaries we believe we are justified in thinking, speaking, and acting certain ways—even if that means stomping on someone else's feelings.

Truly, boundaries and willfulness cannot coexist. If I act willfully, I act without boundaries. They cannot be together, just like light and darkness cannot occupy the same space. And what is willfulness? Nothing less than the seeds of pride. When we get to the point where we see only one choice, one option, we are becoming willful. "It has to be this way," or "No! We will talk about this now!" or "I had to grab him. He wasn't going to give me the TV remote," are examples of being willful.

The rigidity we must exhibit to ensure that things happen our way creates a wall around us. Our willfulness creates a false illusion of safety/protection from whatever impact we imagine *not* getting our way will have on us. Without intact, functional boundaries, the situation is no longer about respecting others or ourselves, about love, about mutual safety or acting in a healthy manner. The interaction is now about protecting a fear, feeding an ego, or gaining control. The rigid barrier we have put around us is pride, which cankers and poisons our actions.

To prove that point, Doug opened the Book of Mormon and read 2 Nephi 28:31: "Cursed is he that putteth his trust in man, or maketh flesh his arm, or shall hearken unto the precepts of men, save their precepts shall be given by the power of the Holy Ghost."

Doug went on to explain that the cost of a willfulness mentality—"my way or the highway"—is nothing short of putting our eternal souls in jeopardy. He read from Mosiah: "But behold, and fear, and tremble before God, for ye ought to tremble; for the Lord redeemeth none such that rebel against him and die in their sins; yea, even all those that have perished in their sins ever since the world began, that have wilfully rebelled against God, that have known the commandments of God, and would not keep them. . . ." (Mosiah 15:26). (Doug stopped and said that boundary failure means that I take the reins and basically tell God, "I think I'd better take over. I know you want me to do it this way, but I think my way is better.") ". . . These are they that have no part in the first resurrection. Therefore ought ye not to tremble? For salvation cometh to none such; for the Lord hath redeemed none such; yea, neither can the Lord redeem such; for he cannot deny himself; for he cannot deny justice when it has its claim" (vv. 26–27).

Salvation cannot be given to those that willfully go after their own way. Why? Because unless one is accessing the Atonement and receiving mercy and forgiveness, there is only one other option left, and that is justice. Justice does not have the power to redeem.

Doug read one more verse: "Having gone according to their own carnal wills and desires; having never called upon the Lord while the arms of mercy were extended towards them; for the arms of mercy were extended towards them, and they would not" (Mosiah 16:12). ("I'm not going to open myself up, become vulnerable with God. I can't let go of doing it my way in order to reach out and grasp His outstretched hands. It's too risky.") "They being warned of their iniquities and yet they would not depart from them; and they were commanded to repent and yet they would not repent." (And what is repentance? To change course or direction. Basically, God is telling me there is another way, a better way to be safe or to gain self-esteem or receive love and validation. Yet I am not going to change course. My way has worked this long. Why should I change?) "And now, ought ye not to tremble and repent of your sins, and remember that only in and through Christ ye can be saved?" (v. 13).

Doug looked over at me and motioned to the verse he had just read. "This verse explains that only through Christ can we be saved, fixed, healed, and freed. Managing my childhood abuse or my marriage or my parenting my way (acting boundary-less) will never offer healing or calm or lasting peace."

If we are to love our neighbor or care for those around us in any way other than in a codependent manner, we must break the cycle of using our own means to deal with wounds (fears) we have inside our souls. When we are willful or controlling, we have lost the ability to act in a healthy manner. Only God can heal our wounds.

What sense does it make to stay willful and not hand the reins over to the Lord, especially when our control and willfulness only create illusions of safety? When conflict comes, and it will, becoming willful kills the ability to treat someone with kindness, respect, understanding, or love. We cannot remain prideful and willful and claim to be followers of Christ.

The only way to break this selfish cycle is by making a conscious decision to turn to the Lord, asking Him how to do it His way. That turning helps us to get centered and begin to rebuild the boundaries that have crumbled around us. This turning actually allows us to partake of the Atonement of Christ. Lehi said as much to his son Jacob: "Behold, he offereth himself a sacrifice for sin, to answer the ends of the law, unto all those who have a broken heart and a contrite spirit; and unto none else can the ends of the law be answered" (2 Nephi 2:7).

I will end with some general points from my discussion with Doug. This is hard work, but I promise it is worth every teardrop and every ounce of frustration. My change of heart is one of my most precious gifts from God.

- I have boundary failure when I am willful.
- I can only connect with or have access to the Atonement when my boundaries are intact.
- The first thing restored to us in the healing process and the repentance process is agency.

- There is no love if there is force.
- Internal control fosters love. Attempting to exert external control (outside of me) diminishes and destroys love.
- Willfulness keeps us stuck in the problem—in the pain.
- Ultimately, the only way to be freed from being frozen in survivor mode is through the Savior.
- You can't be healed when you take control.

PART 5
CREATING THE FUNCTIONAL ADULT

And the Lord said unto me: Marvel not that all mankind, yea, men and women, all nations, kindreds, tongues and people, must be born again; yea, born of God, changed from their carnal and fallen state, to a state of righteousness, being redeemed of God, becoming his sons and daughters;

And thus they become new creatures; and unless they do this, they can in nowise inherit the kingdom of God.

Mosiah 27:25–26

CHAPTER 23

THE FUNCTIONAL ADULT

In chapter 1, we reviewed five traits of codependency as outlined by Pia Mellody. These traits need to be identified and worked on to help create a functional, healthy adult. As the codependent person overcomes these stumbling blocks, the functional adult is born and the individual becomes free of his or her codependency. Looking at each category Mellody outlined, here are some examples of what it might look like to master these deficits:

CODEPENDENT TRAIT	OVERCOMING CODEPENDENT TRAIT
Difficulty with loving oneself	Individual comes to love himself or herself, accepting imperfections as a part of life (see 2 Nephi 2:21).
Difficulty protecting oneself	Person gains ability to protect self better—is able to say "no" and maintain strong, healthy boundaries (see D&C 3:6–7).
Difficulty with self-care	Person takes care of himself or herself—knows his or her needs, understands them, and seeks to have them met without fear or guilt (see 3 Nephi 14:7–11).
Difficulty with self-identity and sharing oneself with others	Individual finds and owns an identity separate from spouse, parents, etc. (Alma 24:7) Individual achieves integration of emotional and intellectual parts of the self—feeling and thinking—allowing both parts to guide in decision making (see D&C 64:34).

CODEPENDENT TRAIT	OVERCOMING CODEPENDENT TRAIT
Difficult time experiencing and expressing one's reality in moderation	Person learns discretion and discernment—knows what to share, who is safe and appropriate to share with, and the appropriate time to share (see 3 Nephi 14:6 and 24:18). Person finds balanced living by maintaining moderation—decrease of the drama, chaos, and stress of daily living; willing to find peace and serenity by giving up the old patterns (see Mosiah 4:27).

FUNCTIONAL ADULT TRAITS

The following is a list of functional behaviors and attitudes for adults. Clearly, we need a new way of living in order to achieve this healthy, mature state.

- Accepts responsibility
- Is honest with self and others
- Can maintain intimate relationships with others
- Has firm boundaries in place
- Allows others to be where they are and is comfortable with the phrase "Things are exactly as they need to be right now."
- Believes in simply doing the best he or she can, rather than in perfectionism
- Is not ruled and motivated by shame and guilt
- Accepts the need for introspection and is willing to change if needed
- Is willing to deal with and work through wounds of the past
- Shows empathy and love for self and others

The creation of the functional adult, which will break the templates and patterns of codependency, requires a set of new skills—new definitions and new ways of looking at life. The new skills, living a new way with Christ as our leader (instead of ourselves, our parents, spouse, boyfriend/girlfriend, or the adversary), requires that we actually practice these skills and implement them in our lives. Otherwise, we will slip back into the old, well-worn patterns of codependency. The Savior declared:

Therefore, whoso heareth these sayings of mine and doeth them, I will liken him unto a wise man, who built his house upon a rock—

And the rain descended, and the floods came, and the winds blew, and beat upon that house; and it fell not, for it was founded upon a rock.

And every one that heareth these sayings of mine and doeth them not shall be likened unto a foolish man, who built his house upon the sand—

And the rain descended, and the floods came, and the winds blew, and beat upon that house; and it fell, and great was the fall of it. (3 Nephi 14:24–27)

One of the first things we need to change is our beliefs. What we believe becomes what we do. In our codependent state, we had many distorted, false, and twisted beliefs. President George Albert Smith said, "If you cross to the devil's side of that line one inch you are in the tempter's power and if he is successful, you will not be able to think or even reason properly because you will have lost the Spirit of the Lord" (G. A. Smith 1948, 43). Without the Spirit guiding us, we are willful, wounded, and afraid, so it is easy to see why we act in such a crazy manner. We must discover our secret, hidden, unspoken beliefs. We need to do away with faulty ideas about the true nature of God. We must throw away our counterfeit notions about grace, vulnerability, charity, and intimacy. We need to discard false beliefs about the Atonement, about how to be a true Latter-day Saint. And in place of all these lies, we will adopt new beliefs.

THE FUNCTIONAL ADULT BELIEF SYSTEM

A functional adult believes the following, as adapted from the writings of Stephen Prior (Prior 1996):

- I have more than two choices—being a victim or a victimizer. I have a third choice in life. I can be a survivor. I am a child of God, and that gives me power and protection.
- I can be vulnerable around safe people because God is with me and will let me know who is safe. I can identify with God, Jesus Christ, or prophets in the scriptures to teach me how to handle opposition in all things.
- I can accept the powerlessness of my childhood. I can tell the truth about my abusers—they caused the trauma and were one hundred percent responsible for it. It is their badness that I felt. I am not bad or evil. I was an innocent little child. I came from God's presence—there was no evil or badness in me.

- I can turn to God for love and nurturing contact. I do not have to repeat the pattern taught to me by my abusers of how to connect to and love someone. That pattern was perverse and wasn't true or right.

- I am something—I am a being of great worth and value. I know that because I am a child of God. I can choose to replace the old, internalized people and patterns with loving Heavenly Parents. Then the very essence of who I am can change from being evil and destructive to being good.

- There are many ways to look at the abuse now. I can sit with the reality of what happened, because I no longer have to rely on the people that hurt me. I can tell the truth of what happened and still be safe. Who I am is completely separate from what happened to me. I look to God, not my abusers, to tell me who I am.

- There was a time when I thought I had to do bad things to get "love" from my abusers. I had to be the way they were with me when they showed their "love" toward me (engage in sexual contact, be mean, be aggressive, etc.).

- My anger and rage at what happened to me has nothing to do with why the abuse happened to me. I have a right to feel angry at the way I was treated.

- God will teach me a better way—how to connect to people, how to love, and how to see myself. He will help me to accept the truth of what was, and what is today. He will heal the hurt, scared little child within me. He will help me to love and accept all parts of me, bringing me to a state of wholeness and health. I can become who I was created to be.

TOOLS OF THE FUNCTIONAL ADULT: BEING PRESENT, NURTURING ONESELF, AND LEARNING TO BE LOVING

To overcome childhood wounds and live in a state of what Stephen Wolinski termed "present accepted-ness," we need to form a functional-adult state to "parent" or take control of present situations, instead of allowing these other, immature parts of us to run the show. Finding that state of "present accepted-ness" means that adults learn to take responsibility for themselves and feel a sense of comfortableness with that responsibility.

As Wolinski states, "Feeling *current* restores one's sense of personal power and enhances one's ability to take responsibility for the ongoing moments of [present] experience(s). An experience once resisted persists until the person is willing to 'experience the experience'" (Wolinski 1991, 24; emphasis in original).

The Savior taught the Saints in the New World that meditation was essential to understanding His doctrine: "Therefore, go ye unto your homes, and ponder upon the things which I have said, and ask of the Father, in my name, that ye may understand, and prepare your minds for the morrow, and I come unto you again" (3 Nephi 17:3). Applying that doctrine is essential to becoming a functional being. Pondering and meditating helps a person to be present (connected to the here and now), and to integrate life lessons.

The struggle many of us face, however, is getting lost in anxiety-fueled thoughts and worries about the future. To be present, in the moment, or meditate is hard to do when we are filled with fears and insecurities about some future event. This does not have to be about something huge looming over us, like a surgery or the loss of a job. It can be as simple as not being able to sleep on a Sunday night because we are worried about this appointment or that meeting later in the week. President Harold B. Lee counseled: "Don't try to live too many days ahead. Seek for strength to attend to the problems of today. In his Sermon on the Mount, the Master admonished: 'Take therefore no thought for the morrow: for the morrow shall take thought for the things of itself. Sufficient unto the day is the evil thereof' (Matthew 6:34)" (Lee 1971).

Nurturing

As a wounded adult stuck in either a dependent or needless state, it is easy to be confused about how to nurture oneself. And rightly so. Being in either state keeps us trapped—frozen in the past, looking at nurturing from a child's perspective. From a child's perspective, nurturing is left largely up to the primary caretaker. As children grow, finding ways to self-nurture begins to occur, i.e., sucking their thumbs, wrapping themselves in a favorite blanket, or simply being in tune to their bodies—eating when hungry, sleeping when tired, laughing when happy.

Yet many wounded adults, in their child states, clamor to be seen and are anxious and extra vigilant about having someone else meet their needs. Removing the anxiety, the fear, and the unpredictability of life becomes the reason to find nurturing. True nurturing doesn't happen and is not pursued because the individual doesn't know what it looks like or feels like. Left to themselves, these wounded adults find shortcuts to soothing. Nurturing becomes equated with stuffing emotions, connecting to the thrill or adrenaline of life, doing anything in a compulsive manner (cleaning, eating, having sex, doing crafts, chatting on the internet, etc.), and isolating. "Unfortunately, these are counterfeit forms of self-comfort because they stimulate us. Healthy self-soothing calms the nervous system and stills our minds" (Kasl 2001, 48).

Being emotionally dependent on someone else is not an indication of nurturing. Having someone take care of your daily decisions is not nurturing. Having someone work at diffusing your anger or other intense emotions is not nurturing. Trying to get someone to love you is not a form of nurturing.

So, what is nurturing? Nurturing is nonsexual touch—a hug, snuggling, scratching a back, massaging someone's head. Nurturing is the soothing behaviors parents do with infants—cooing, singing softly, rocking in a rocking chair. Nurturing is tucking the little seven-year-old in bed, reading her a story, and kissing her gently on the forehead. Nurturing is curling up in a big blanket and reading a book. Nurturing is affirming yourself. Nurturing is taking a bubble bath. Nurturing is taking care of the bumps and scrapes little Johnny gets as he falls off his bike—without the harsh "I told you to go slower!" Nurturing is taking a nap when you're sleepy. Nurturing is brushing your teeth and wearing clean clothes and getting a haircut. Nurturing is eating healthily. Nurturing is going to a recovery group and allowing the group to validate your progress.

Whatever the behaviors, nurturing oneself requires the person to be in the present. Attempting to be more present, more rooted and grounded, more integrated as a person is itself a form of nurturing.

How can you become more present? Try some of the following suggestions to help bring a calming, grounded sensation to your body.

- Rub your ears. Massage them, following the curves and dips. First do one ear, then the other. Put all your focus and attention into the physical sensation of touching your ears.
- Cross your arms and pat your shoulders with your hands, alternating between the right shoulder and then the left one. This is called the butterfly technique. While you do this, softly repeat a positive affirmation, such as "I am a capable adult who is full of resources," or "I am lovable just the way I am," or "My body is a safe place where my head and heart can be together." Do this for ten minutes.
- When you take a shower, take time to center on each part of your body. Allow yourself to completely focus on washing your hair. Find descriptive words to

explain and describe what it feels like to wash your hair. Spend a few minutes really focusing on washing your feet. Embrace the physical reaction to washing your feet. Notice the curves of the bones, the way each toe is shaped, how your heel looks and feels to the touch. Repeat with other parts of your body.

- Take your thumb and middle finger to gently hold the bridge of your nose. Then take your second finger and gently tap just below where your eyebrows would meet in the middle. Do that for a few minutes, focusing on your breathing. Then move to either side of your eyes—your temple region—and massage them slowly, again focusing on your breath.

How does Father in Heaven nurture us? He comforts us through the Holy Ghost. He speaks to us from the pages of holy scripture. He speaks to us through His servants—the President of the Church, and the other Apostles and General Authorities. Heavenly Father speaks peace to us, showers us with His love, and reassures us that He is there. He infuses us with heavenly hope. He applies the balm of Gilead to our wounded souls. He does not reveal all things to us at once or always tell us what is going to happen in the future. He does not always take the struggle from us.

His nurturing and comforting is present oriented—rooted and grounded in the here and now. He doesn't undo the past but instead helps us to learn from it, overcome the stumbling blocks that formed in the past, and grow from past negative experiences.

This nurturing and comforting helps us to find lasting peace and joy. Lehi explains that "Adam fell that men might be [exist, gain a physical body, live and die, and experience this mortal world]; and men are, that they might have joy" (2 Nephi 2:25). Yet this joy does not come from man, nor does man have the power to create this state of rejoicing. Lehi taught that this joy only comes through the "merits, and mercy, and grace of the Holy Messiah" (2 Nephi 2:8). In fact, the main message of the Church's twelve-step program is that through the Atonement of Jesus Christ, our very nature can change. That is what gives us lasting change. That is what gives us charity and compassion for ourselves and others. It is the great sacrifice of our Savior that comforts us perfectly—and gives us joy.

Loving

Instead of loving, the wounded adult controls, coerces, manipulates, and forces. Learning to love instead of controlling is an essential lesson in becoming a functional adult. But many people don't have the skills or knowledge to interact in a loving (not dysfunctional or addictive) manner. The following list of ways to show love to others is adapted from Patrick Carnes's work (Carnes 1997). Notice that these are small acts, but that each requires conscious thought and the ability to be present—to be able to notice and see the loving acts of your partner.

- *Affirming love behaviors.* Acts that show we enjoy and appreciate our partner and that show moral and emotional support.
- *Expressing love behaviors.* Using our tone of voice, gestures, body language, and facial expressions to show our love.
- *Verbal love behaviors.* Using words, pet names, and phrases that show our love.
- Self-disclosing love behaviors. Being open and vulnerable with our partner— sharing intimate details.
- *Tolerating love behaviors.* Accepting less-pleasant aspects of our partner in a nonjudgmental way.
- *Tactile love behavior.* Physical affection, snuggling, hugging, holding hands, gentle caresses, etc.
- *Gift love behaviors.* Giving gifts that demonstrate how much we care for our partner.
- *Receptional love behaviors.* Acknowledging gratitude when these behaviors are done to us. This can happen by doing the following:
  - ° Actively identifying and focusing on each expression of love as shown by your partner.
  - ° Avoiding putting down or ignoring the expression of love when you notice it.
  - ° Giving appropriate comments showing you did notice and appreciate the expression of love.

In this chapter, we have explored several tools for helping create a functional adult within each of us. For many, these tools and exercises will feel clumsy and perhaps even uncomfortable. Indeed, these tools may even be the exact opposite of what many have experienced in their growing-up years. So, remember the mantra of practice and patience, practice and patience, practice and patience.

As President Dieter F. Uchtdorf reminds us: "Heavenly Father wants us to become more like him . . . God understands that we get there not in an instant but by taking one step at a time. I do not believe in a God who would set up rules and commandments only to wait for us to fail so He could punish us . . . Even when we stumble, He urges us not to be discouraged—never to give up . . . but to take courage, find our faith and keep trying. Our Father in Heaven mentors His children and often sends unseen heavenly help to those who desire to follow the Savior" (Uchtdorf 2013).

CHAPTER 24

BOUNDARIES

All children need to know they are safe. All children need to know they are loved. All children need to know they can rely on their primary caretakers to meet their needs and protect them. If this happens, the parents are honoring the child's boundaries. Boundaries are the invisible containers that help an individual to gain a sense of self. If we could see them, boundaries would be, as Pia Mellody calls it, a second skin. They protect the person from other people's emotions and help the individual contain his or her own emotions.

If I have my boundaries intact and someone is crying, I can have empathy and show support, but I won't "own" that emotion. I won't end up going to the same place where the crying person is. With firm boundaries, I won't have my emotions spill out onto other people—and I will remain connected to myself and my feelings.

Charles Whitfield highlights this with the following chart from his book *Boundaries and Relationships* (Whitfield 1994):

HEALTHY BOUNDARIES

What Is Mine

My awareness of my inner life
My inner life, including my beliefs, thoughts, feelings, decisions, choices,
    experiences, wants, needs, and unconscious material
My behavior
The responsibility to make my life successful and joyful

Others' awareness of their inner lives

Material from others' inner lives, including their beliefs, thoughts, feelings, decisions, choices, experiences, wants, needs, and unconscious material

Others' behavior

Others' responsibility to make their lives successful and joyful

TEACHING BY EXAMPLE

Children are born with boundaries, but they need to learn how to use them. This type of learning comes from their parents in two ways—by watching and by experiencing. Children observe constantly. They see what their parents do. In turn, children mimic and mirror the adult behavior. This is how a child learns to walk, talk, and interact with others. *If a child's parents have poor boundaries, the child will have poor boundaries.*

One example comes from a client when asked how he got so good at putting people down. He said he would listen to his parents and how they talked about other people. During dinner, it was very common for them to make negative and critical comments about fat people, lower-class people, and unemployed people. It became a habit, and this man became very adept at tearing others down.

Another client said that when she first met her future family-in-law, her fiancé's brothers walked around in their underwear. "Here I was, meeting my future husband's family. I wake up and come down for breakfast, and I am shocked at what I see. His brothers were walking around in their underwear and nothing else, eating breakfast and chatting, with no sense of impropriety. They acknowledged me, but didn't run and put on a robe or clothes. They got out cereal for me and showed me where the milk was—all the while in their Fruit of the Loom underwear. I was so embarrassed."

CREATION OF THE SELF

Boundaries create a sense of self. A sense of self helps people to interact with others with calm and inner confidence. A lack of boundaries requires the person to seek a sense of self outside of himself or herself—like a balloon needing someone to fill it up with air. Partial boundaries or no boundaries at all are a common characteristic for someone who struggles with codependency.

The less defined a person's boundaries are, the less likely he or she is to have a sense of self. With that comes a disbelief in one's worth and value. When boundaries are violated, the sense of self is decimated, hence the need to try to overcome the violation and regain a sense of self. Life without a sense of self is akin to eating without taste—living becomes a boring, empty drudgery. Until recovery happens, the attempt to regain the self is made through addictive and compulsive patterns.

What that does is set up the wounded adult's need to have others define him or her and provide a sense of self. Therefore, all it takes is for someone to be nice to, polite to, acknowledge, or strike up a conversation to get the wounded adult believing that you see something of value in them. The wounded individual's knee-jerk reaction is to latch onto anyone who pays positive attention to him or her. Since the codependent has little of himself or herself to give (since there is rarely a sense of self in the first place), attachments to others are often created by intensity and intrigue. A person coming to a pool of water in the desert probably won't stop to think about whether or not the water is clean and pure. Likewise, a wounded adult often won't even ask himself or herself whether or not the person he or she is latching onto is dangerous.

VIOLATING BOUNDARIES

Children also learn through experience. One way they learn about boundaries is by experiencing their parents' respect or disregard for their boundaries. Physical abuse, emotional abuse, and sexual abuse are just a few of the ways a parent can violate a child's boundaries. Stories of abuse, in any and all forms, are common as codependents tell their stories. The aftermath of these horrific boundary violations is seen in the way the codependent interacts with others: he or she will either compulsively act out the violation in some form, or compulsively withdraw from any kind of behavior that even remotely resembles the past behavior.

Having a parent with poor boundaries is another common characteristic of codependents. The father who discloses his sexual thoughts and experiences to his son or daughter, the mother who has her seven-year-old son take baths with her, the mother who leans on her daughter or son for emotional support, or the father who rages to intimidate the family—all are examples of boundary failure on the part of the parent. It comes as no surprise that the child grows up with a twisted and distorted sense of what is appropriate and acceptable.

Often, the wounded individual subconsciously tries to re-create the original damaged relationship with others. If the person had an enmeshed, boundary-less relationship with the opposite-sex parent, more often than not, as an adult the codependent will create enmeshed boundary-less relationships with other opposite-sex partners. Having poor boundaries, one is set up to either continue to reenact the trauma or to completely disengage from others. Both responses are compulsive and make up the scenery that is called addiction. More subtle but just as detrimental to boundaries is the parent who is overly critical, who rarely shows any physical affection to the child, who treats the child like a mini grown-up, or who rarely interacts with the child.

If a parent violates a child's boundaries, the child is going to have weak, damaged boundaries, or if the violations happen often, no boundaries at all. This leaves the child feeling unsafe. Vulnerability becomes a deficit. Trust becomes difficult to receive or give. The sense of self within the child becomes hampered and sometimes lost. The child will get wounded—emotionally, physically, mentally, sexually, and spiritually. Far too often, these are the experiences children have as they grow up in this mortal, fallen world.

A wounded child can remain in that state of pain and hurt and fear for only so long. He or she usually learns to adapt—to survive. For example, living with a raging alcoholic, a child will adapt and learn to watch his or her father very closely, and if the child notices the tell-tale signs, he or she will run and hide. Growing up, the child will become finely attuned to others' emotions and behaviors, remaining disconnected from his or her own emotional state. Anger becomes a trigger to leave or run away or emotionally withdraw.

Adaptation usually involves a splitting off of or disconnection from emotions and from the authentic self. Since the child perceives these things as vulnerabilities, the adapted part of the personality decides they are too dangerous to have. The adapted part of the child is focused solely on survival, and with time, the adaptation becomes more and more adaptive and innovative. This is the source of addiction and a host of mental health disorders.

BOUNDARIES AND INTIMACY

Typically, a person who struggles with relationships has few or no boundaries and is therefore exposed to others' thoughts, feelings, and behaviors. Often, the converse is also true—the person has thick walls that protect him or her to the point that there is no connection with others. As the recovering person goes to twelve-step meetings and works with a sponsor, a therapist, and others, the individual will be asked to open up and share intimate thoughts, feelings, and details of his or her life. If the person lets down those walls, he or she is left totally unprotected. If he or she has no boundaries to begin with, the individual will feel easily overwhelmed and emotionally wrung out. What is needed is an understanding of boundaries as the person begins this journey of self-reflection and recovery. Boundaries should be one of the first tools we pick up and learn how to use.

Some people have trouble understanding what a personal boundary is—what it looks like and feels like. I often ask clients to visualize putting on their boundaries, like a second skin. Some people imagine their boundaries as a wetsuit. Others visualize a force field. One individual saw his boundaries as made of armor, while another saw them as a suit made of woven flowers. Whenever there was a difficult conversation to have with someone else in the therapy session, we would stop, visualize putting on our boundaries, take a couple of deep breaths, and proceed. This is especially needed in marriage work, when emotions such as fear, anger, and confusion run high.

Some people have trouble visualizing their boundaries. This is okay. One recovering codependent explained that she could only visualize her boundaries coming up to her chest, leaving her upper body and head fully exposed. She was afraid that having a boundary over her heart would keep her from connecting with others—and therefore keep her lonely. She was accustomed to losing herself in others, and she didn't know how to connect any other way. As she progressed in recovery, her boundaries were eventually able to protect all of her. Her relationships became much more healthy and much less filled with drama.

Pia Mellody uses the metaphor of a flap or door in one's boundaries over the heart, as a way to open up to others. The doorknob is on the inside, so the individual is always in charge of whether or not to open that door and allow other people's thoughts in. In this way, a person can be vulnerable and still be protected. In fact, when it comes to vulnerability as a component of intimacy, it is not about letting down personal boundaries, but about each individual maintaining his or her own identity and sense of self as the two people share their thoughts and feelings with each other.

SIGNS OF HEALTHY BOUNDARIES

In trying to achieve codependent sobriety, finding what "right" or "healthy" looks like can be difficult. Why? Because so much of this journey happens internally. And since so few of us have an example to reflect on, it can be a daunting task to know when we are interacting and thinking from a healthy place. Let's end this chapter with some practical snapshots of what healthy boundaries look like. The following list is adapted from a lecture by Pia Mellody (Mellody 2002).

- Appropriate trust
- Revealing a little of yourself at a time, checking to see how the other person responds to your sharing
- Moving step by step into intimacy
- Putting a new acquaintanceship on hold until you check for compatibility
- Deciding whether a potential relationship will be good for you
- Staying focused on your own growth and recovery
- Maintaining personal values despite what others want
- Noticing when someone else displays inappropriate boundaries
- Noticing when someone invades your boundaries
- Saying no to food, gifts, touch, and sex that you don't want
- Asking a person before touching him or her
- Respect for others—not taking advantage of someone's generosity
- Self-respect—not giving too much in hope that someone will like you
- Trusting your own decisions
- Knowing who you are and what you want
- Recognizing that friends and partners are not mind-readers
- Clearly communicating your wants and needs (and also recognizing and accepting that you may be turned down and not get what you want)
- Talking to yourself with gentleness, humor, love, and respect

CHAPTER 25

COMMUNICATION

In *Codependent No More,* Melody Beattie explains what communication looks like for those in an addictive state. "We carefully choose our words to manipulate, people please, control, cover up, and alleviate guilt. Our communication reeks of repressed feelings, repressed thoughts, ulterior motives, low self-worth, and shame . . . We don't say what we mean; we don't mean what we say" (Beattie 1986, 23).

The way we communicate with others can be a key indicator that we are acting from a wounded, codependent state. The scriptures often tie the way we communicate to our spiritual state (see Doctrine and Covenants 136:23–24; Alma 12:14). Peter said we should "refrain [our] tongue from evil, and [our] lips that they speak no guile" (1 Peter 3:10).

The following examples of communicating from a dysfunctional state were adapted from Charlotte Kasl's work (Kasl 2001).

- Focusing the conversation back to you
- Analyzing—taking the conversation from an emotional level to a left-brain analysis
- Shifting the topic to someone else other than the person speaking with you
- Not responding at all
- Making patronizing statements—"Everyone goes through that," "You'll be all right," or "There is nothing to worry about."
- Responding with platitudes—"God never gives you more than you can handle," or "You'll look back on this and see how much you've grown."
- Changing the subject completely
- Interrupting to ask unimportant details

In recovery, we operate from a place of "rigorous honesty" with ourselves first, and then with others. This basic shift drastically changes how we communicate. We no longer use our speech to attempt to seduce, manipulate, or coerce. Instead, we honestly express our thoughts and feelings and state our needs clearly. Learning to do this takes time—time to reconnect to our feelings and break through the haze of self-deception.

The idea is to slow down and recognize what is happening in your body and mind. So much of what you've done in terms of communicating comes from a well-worn pattern and distorted belief system. At first this may feel awkward and slow, but remember—you are learning and discovering, perhaps for the first time, how to communicate from a place of honesty and self-awareness. When you do this the relationship will change, and how you deal with problems will change. It will look something like this:

- Each partner acknowledges his or her differences and expresses his or her feelings and wants openly.
- Each partner accepts each other's right to his or her passions, even if the other person can't relate to them.
- Each partner maintains his or her own, separate identity. Neither one sacrifices his or her deeply held values to placate the other. Neither changes his or her behavior simply to placate or try to change the other.
- Each partner does not add layers of interpretations to the other's behaviors—as in "You don't respect me when you do that," or "If you loved me, you'd . . ." or "You're just trying to control me when you . . ."
- Once a decision has been made, each partner lets it go, not dwelling on it, and moves on.
- Each partner then shifts his or her focus to all the ways he or she enjoys and appreciates the other person.

Sharing thoughts and feelings in an honest, appropriate manner is the first step in correcting addictive ways of communicating. The next step in changing one's communication style is listening. For an individual who is operating from a codependent state, there is little true listening to another person. Rather, the codependent individual is usually thinking of comebacks, creating cover-ups, or figuring out how to fix a problem.

Real listening requires the listener to remain in the moment, present and focused on the other person. But someone who operates from a codependent state is focused solely on his or her own needs and wants, looking forward to the time where he or she gets to talk, share, and get personal needs met.

The following anonymous poem sums up how to listen effectively:

Listen

When I ask you to listen to me and you start to give advice, you have not done what I asked.

When I ask you to listen to me and you begin to tell me why I shouldn't feel that way, you are trampling on my feelings.

When I ask you to listen to me and you believe you have to do something to solve my problem, you have failed me, strange as it may seem.

Listen. All I asked was that you listen, not talk or do—just hear me.

Rarely is a codependent positioned in the present. This is because doing so would require him or her to "just be," to quiet the chaos within and truly connect with someone else. This basic requirement for listening and sharing is a necessary ingredient for intimacy. Only healing the wounds that created a person's codependency can help him or her to feel safe and comfortable in talking and listening from a place of true intimacy. "As we share our fears, they tend to reduce in size, and fall into proportion. The parts of our fears that are irrational and therefore cause anxiety become clearer" (Dayton 2007, 169)

From that place of healing, the way partners interact with each other changes. They can honestly state what their needs are, say what they are feeling and thinking, and still retain their sense of self. "People feel an internal steadiness and an ability to voice their needs, so that intimacy does not carry the risk of being swallowed up. Each person has a safe internal home to return to. Both partners are attentive to not treating their mate as an object to fulfill their needs" (Kasl 2001, 121).

Healing and recovery is first about stopping self-destructive behaviors. Second, it offers something or someone solid for us to hold onto (God, friends, a therapist, etc.) while we learn new behaviors and skills. Third, recovery works at helping us heal our wounds and restores our belief in our inner worth and value. Finally, recovery teaches us how to build bridges with others—how to form healthy and honest relationships.

Chapter 26

Integration, Wholeness, and Resiliency

As individuals who struggle with codependency begin to incorporate these concepts into their lives, they will gain a greater variety of functional skills. They will grow emotionally and mentally. In turn, this whole process will increase their maturity. They will become more centered, grounded, and secure with themselves. When there are events that trigger the adapted state to take charge of a given situation (slipping us back into a trance state—those well-worn templates), the functional adult can work with the wounded-child state to meet his or her present needs instead of reverting to the old, dysfunctional survival skills. Claudia Black offers five core recovery skills for creating a functional adult (Black 1993).

1. Validate yourself
2. Let go of some control
3. Feel your feelings
4. Identify your needs
5. Set limits and boundaries

This list reflects skills children gain when they have experienced secure attachment. With time, the functional adult will be able to incorporate the wounded-child state. The adaptive-child state will no longer need to maintain the security of one's psyche; rather, the strength, perseverance, and problem-solving skills of the adaptive-child states will be integrated within the functional adult. Integration is supported by the following behaviors:

•   Being creative and exploring your creativity, being flexible and exploring
    your flexibility, being active, being curious, enhancing your social skills,

acting cooperatively, working at connecting to a peer group, being able to use soothing memories to offset troubling ones, being able to reconstruct how you talk about your life, and being able to have a more comprehensive narrative about your life instead of being so fragmented (Punämaki 2002).

- Working on adopting stress management techniques, relaxation skills, and addressing thought distortions (Cohen 2004).

- Being consistent with yourself and others. Telling yourself you'll do something and then doing it.

- Listening to and talking with your inner child. Talking to that part of you, that wounded little boy or girl, and getting a sense of how that part of you is feeling and thinking.

- Practicing nondominant dialogues with yourself. *Recovery of Your Inner Child,* by Lucia Capacchione, Ph.D., is an excellent resource for those wanting to try these types of exercises.

- Telling your inner child that all feelings are okay.

- Practicing putting words to feelings—learning to label emotions.

- Teaching your inner child about God. Offer "all of you" a chance to receive a testimony. Don't let your spirituality remain compartmentalized like your emotions.

- Remembering the three A's—awareness, acceptance, and action. Awareness comes by experiencing previously blocked emotions and processing the associated thoughts and beliefs. Acceptance involves understanding and realizing the impact in various areas of your life. This is also the place where many levels of denial are broken and the person begins to deal with the reality of his or her life—as things really were. Action denotes resolving the past, integrating the old and the new.

FOSTERING RESILIENCY

No more victim or aggressor templates. No more martyr templates. No more fear-of-abandonment patterns. No more codependent templates. In a functional state, we become survivors. We become assertive. We become strong, confident individuals. The past no longer defines us, and past wounds no longer poison us. We are not passive. We are going to act, not be acted upon (see 2 Nephi 2). We are going to become resilient.

Resilient Qualities

Tian Dayton explains that a resilient person is:

- Inventive
- Creative
- Courageous
- Dogged
- Humorous
- Self-reliant
- Independent
- Loyal
- Spiritual (Dayton 2007, 255–67)

How to Foster Resiliency

Dayton suggests doing the following to foster resiliency:

- Reframe life issues
- Stay away from "victim thinking"
- Maintain good boundaries
- Develop inner resources—strengthen your inner self
- Don't avoid life
- Find other family models
- Get honest with yourself
- Take meaningful action
- Look for the lessons
- Work through past issues
- Find and maintain relationships (ibid)

From a spiritual point of view, resiliency is akin to faith, to enduring to the end. Finding and exhibiting charity in the face of trials and hardships is never easy. One sister explained how hard it was to love her husband and be charitable towards him when he kept falling back into his addiction. Another sister expressed the difficulty of holding onto charity when the fear of facing her childhood abuse kept hardening her heart. President Henry B. Eyring declared, "If the foundation of faith is not embedded in our hearts, the power to endure will crumble" (Eyring 2012). He lists the traits on which we need to build that foundation (or in other words—create resiliency): hard work, patience, personal integrity, choosing the right consistently, having faith in the right person—Christ—serving and forgiving others (ibid). Not surprisingly, the very traits that build resiliency are the characteristics of charity. Seeking charity will create resiliency in us. The pure love of God, as it is found within us, will give us that sure foundation, keeping us immovable and steadfast in the face of trials and adversity (see Helaman 5:12).

In the end, meeting the needs of those discounted and disowned parts of ourselves leads to change and happiness. As Robert Burney put it: "Nothing you do in your life will be more rewarding or have more far reaching consequences than healing your wounded soul—which is what your wounded inner children represent. We are—you are, I am—lovable and worthy" (Burney 1995, 157).

I have seen grown adults cry like small children, begging for their mommy to love them. I have seen a brother in the gospel bellow and scream and hit a cushion, all the while asking over and over why he wasn't good enough for his dad. I have seen women talk to these little disowned parts of themselves with loving kindness and feel the room fill up with the spirit of love and healing. I watched while one young man held himself—wrapping his arms around himself—with tears streaming down his face as he said, "I am lovable, even in my weaknesses."

I have witnessed the healing power of God's love. I have experienced the *aha* moments where enlightenment opens eyes and realizations hit home with the power to change behavior. I have felt the Holy Ghost lead, guide, and direct myself and others on this path towards finding Christ. At times, I have such an overwhelming sense of love from Heavenly Father, I can feel the ministering of angels. I have shouted for joy with those who have overcome. I have wept with those who have let go of their dreams and accepted the reality of their pasts. Truly, God is a God of miracles.

CHAPTER 27

CODEPENDENT SOBRIETY

The codependent template in chapter 10 is only half of the equation. The other half outlines how you can be healthy and remain connected to God. In the diagram on page 146, notice that you become more and receive more (freedom, spiritual gifts and abilities) when you turn to Heavenly Father to help you deal with life. And conversely, you receive less and become less as you turn to your own ways to manage life.

From this place of action, having faith and turning to God, you are blessed with the following skills and gifts:

- Boundaries
- Ability to remain grounded
- Ability to remain in a functional adult place (emotionally, intellectually, spiritually)
- Ability to access your talents and resources
- Ability to experience calm
- Restored agency, since you are no longer stuck or trapped in old, dysfunctional patterns

President Ezra Taft Benson taught: "Men and women who turn their lives over to God will discover that He can make a lot more out of their lives than they can. He will deepen their joys, expand their vision, quicken their minds, strengthen their muscles, lift their spirits, multiply their blessings, increase their opportunities, comfort their souls, raise up friends, and pour out peace" (Benson 1988, 4).

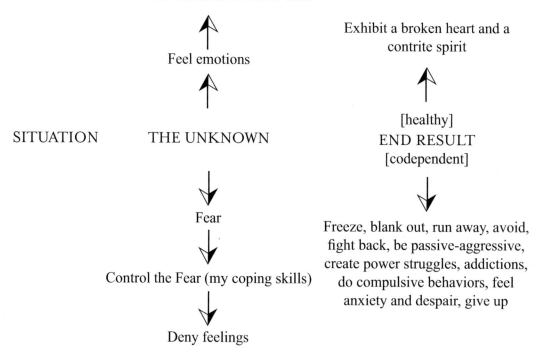

"I know in whom I trust—God."

In order to do something different—make a
healthy choice—I need to see the trigger (what
makes me turn to my coping skills) and make
a conscious decision to turn to God.

Feel emotions

Exhibit a broken heart and a
contrite spirit

SITUATION   THE UNKNOWN

[healthy]
END RESULT
[codependent]

Fear

Control the Fear (my coping skills)

Freeze, blank out, run away, avoid,
fight back, be passive-aggressive,
create power struggles, addictions,
do compulsive behaviors, feel
anxiety and despair, give up

Deny feelings

When you get triggered and go to your coping skills, there is no need for faith and no need to trust God. Your heart becomes hardened. Here are some facts about triggers:

- Triggers are like a knee-jerk reaction (seemingly automatic response) that activates old patterns and behaviors.
- These triggers are held in the fragmented, compartmentalized, dysfunctional parts of you.
- Triggers don't originate from the healthy, authentic, functional self.

Now what? If you don't want to be codependent anymore, what do you do? How do you know what "right" looks like? The rest of this chapter will answer those questions.

Many Latter-day Saints wonder if they are doing service with the right motivation. They ask, "Am I serving to build myself up, or to fix or save others to make myself feel and look better? Am I doing service to build up the kingdom of God and show gratitude to the Savior?" Service is such an integral part of being a member of the Church that it can be difficult to discern our motivations.

As you learn to be more aware of your motives, *do service anonymously,* at least in the beginning. There will be no payoff, no self-esteem boost, no spotlight, no "thank you" or "you're so wonderful." It will help you give service in a non-dysfunctional way. It will be just you and God.

Another way to determine if you are being codependent is to follow this simple saying: "When in doubt, check it out." If you don't know if what you are doing is codependent, check it out. Ask Heavenly Father. Ask a trusted advisor or sponsor. Ask a counselor or therapist.

Al-Anon and Co-Dependents Anonymous (CoDa) use the phrase "Detach with love." At first, this statement may seem contradictory. If I am detaching from someone, that doesn't sound like I love him or her. Recently, the Spirit taught Rex about detaching with love. Rex was worried about his wife and her return to drinking caffeinated soda. This was a problem for her, as she had become addicted to it and suffered from severe migraines if she didn't drink it. She had worked hard at quitting, and the headaches had decreased. Her sleep was better. Rex was afraid all these health problems would return. He started to harp on her and micromanage her. She became angry. He exclaimed to me, "I was being very codependent about the whole thing." He shares the following insight in his own words:

One day, as I struggled with this concept, I decided to pray. The thought came to me, "If your wife is going back to drinking caffeinated soda, and she asks you to go to the store and get her some, express your love to her and then politely say no."

Wow! So simple and easy, and yet I couldn't see it until God pointed it out to me. Instead of trying to control my wife and guilt her and shame her into changing, I realized I had no power over her and that she has her agency. Instead of making a big deal about every time she pops open a can of Diet Pepsi, I can detach from the behavior. I don't let it run my bus. I won't do anything that will enable her to continue her behavior, but I also won't be self-righteous or judgmental about it, either. I won't nitpick. I won't harass her. I won't throw away the soda when she's not looking (which I used to do).

I will show her that I love her. I will snuggle and cuddle with her, and do nice things like clean the kitchen or do the laundry. I will buy her a card or leave little love notes for her. Detaching with love is the equivalent of loving the sinner and hating the sin (and not taking away the sinner's agency to get him or her to stop committing the sin).

A couple of days later, I was reading in 3 Nephi. The Savior was talking to the multitude in the land of Bountiful and said something that made me stop reading. I stared at the page as if He was right there in my bedroom talking to me. "And why beholdest thou the mote that is in thy brother's eye, but considerest not the beam that is in thine own eye? Or how wilt thou say to thy brother: Let me pull the mote out of thine eye—and behold, a beam is in thine own eye? Thou hypocrite, first cast the beam out of thine own eye; and then shalt thou see clearly to cast the mote out of thy brother's eye" (3 Nephi 14:3–5).

I was chastened. I was taught. And I repented. I asked my wife for forgiveness for trying to usurp her agency. Now, whenever I have the knee-jerk reaction to "help" someone change a behavior, I first stop and check in with myself. Am I doing what's right? Am I in good standing with the Lord? And does He even want me to interject, interfere, and intervene?

Let's not forget the other rule of codependent sobriety—*if the person doesn't ask for help, don't give it to them, unless God tells you to.* And even then, try to be as inconspicuous as possible. Quiet, secret service is so much better than knocking on someone's door and holding out two bags of groceries when the person opens the door.

Along those same lines, *if a person isn't asking for your advice, don't give it to them unless God tells you to.* Unsolicited advice rarely goes over well. And even if it's a pearl of wisdom and could really help that person, if he or she isn't in a place to receive it, understand it, and accept it, the only thing that will happen is both of you will end up with hurt feelings.

When someone you love—a spouse, a child, a close friend, a sibling—is doing a dangerous and destructive behavior, setting a boundary is appropriate. *Setting a boundary and then enforcing (following through with) that boundary is how to change a behavior.* Setting a boundary, like everything else we've been talking about, should be done respectfully and clearly. This is not a power play. This is not a control tactic. This is not an "I'm gonna throw this in your face" action. Instead, we draw a line in the sand to show respect to ourselves and the other person. We remain true to our values and morals. We remain honest and upfront.

Here are some examples of setting a clear boundary:

- "No, it is not okay for you to look at pornography on our home computer."
- "I can no longer allow you to come home drunk. If you get drunk, don't come home until you've sobered up."
- "If you bring drugs into this house, I can no longer allow you to live here."
- "If you keep looking at porn on your cell phone, I will stop paying for the phone service."
- "If you go on another food binge, I will leave the room. If you continue to choose food as a way to manage your life, I will need to reevaluate our relationship."
- "When you yell at me and call me names, it hurts my feelings. In the future, when you do that, what I will do to take care of myself is to walk away. If you continue your behavior, I will get in the car and drive away."

Take time to connect with God through the Holy Ghost. Codependent sobriety cannot be found or maintained without Heaven's help. Most often, that help comes from the Holy Ghost. Quoting Parley P. Pratt:

The gift of the Holy Ghost . . . quickens all the intellectual faculties, increases, enlarges, expands, and purifies all the natural passions and affections, and adapts them, by the gift of wisdom, to their lawful use. It inspires, develops, cultivates, and matures all the fine-toned sympathies, joys, tastes, kindred feelings, and affections of our nature. It inspires virtue, kindness, goodness, tenderness, gentleness, and charity. It develops beauty of person, form, and features. It tends to health, vigor, animation, and social feeling. It invigorates all the faculties of the physical and intellectual man. It strengthens and gives tone to the nerves. In short, it is, as it were, marrow to the bone, joy to the heart, light to the eyes, music to the ears, and life to the whole being. (Pratt 2012)

The Holy Ghost offers comfort, soothing and nurturing a wounded soul. Through the Holy Ghost, Heavenly Father fills the emptiness of our hearts—the jagged holes we can never seem to fill ourselves. "For that [the Spirit of God] satisfies and fills up every longing of the human heart. When I am filled with that spirit my soul is satisfied; and I can say in good earnest that trifling things of the day don't seem to stand in my way at all. But just let me lose my hold of that spirit and power of the Gospel and partake of the spirit of the world, in the slightest degree and trouble comes; there is something wrong. I am tried; and what can comfort me? You cannot impart comfort to me . . . but that which comes from the fountain above" (Snow 1874).

It is very common for codependents to slip back into old thinking and old patterns. This is a learning process, and Heavenly Father knows that. He gives us grace—a portion of Christ's power—to allow us to do what we could not normally do on our own. However, many people, even in the Church, have distorted thoughts about grace. Rhonda, a member of a women's group I lead, wrote the following:

> Until now, my interest and understanding of grace was no deeper than remembering the poem "Footprints in the Sand." I thought it was a sweet story. I read 2 Nephi 25:23, where it says that grace comes after everything I can do. So I thought I had to do everything myself.
>
> And then as Doug and I talked, he gave me a new way to look at grace. "Any awareness is grace," he said. "Feeling love is grace. Strength is grace." He went on to tell me that when my heart is closed (being in survival mode) grace is what opens me up. Grace does not protect me from pain or sorrow, but it allows me to endure that pain and sorrow in a healthy, functional way. We then revisited 2 Nephi 25:23. Doug asked, "What is Nephi referring to when he says 'after all we can do?'" Then Doug explained that all we can do is repent—change.
>
> Grace supports us as we seek to repent, to change. Changing course is never pleasant or easy, but grace helps me make it through the difficult transition.
>
> We can't have grace or access it if we are being willful and trying to do things our way. Doug and I reviewed Helaman 4. The people boasted in their own strength and the Lord no longer preserved them (another thing grace does for us—preserves us). Then Doug and I likened this scripture to my codependency. Boasting in my own strength, leaning on myself instead of reaching out and asking for grace—Christ's power—looks like me saying, "I will fix this," or "I know what to say or do."
>
> Through grace, Jesus will heal dysfunctional messages. He will help me to recognize my distorted thoughts and help me to stop fixing everything. Having the Savior's strength and guidance as I deal with challenges is an example of grace.

Don't beat yourself up if you don't get it right the first three hundred times. Remember the adage "It works, if you work it." Keep trying. Keep looking. Keep open. Allow God to show you, teach you, and mold you. He'll do it with love and mercy. He knows better than anyone what codependent sobriety looks like. And He knows how to get us there. Trust Him. Trust the process. Trust the journey.

CHAPTER 28

CHARITY-BASED PARENTING

The family is a social unit that offers protection, support, love, and learning. The concept of family is part of God's plan of happiness and has existed for eons of time. Before we came to earth, we lived as spirit brothers and sisters with our Heavenly Parents. Each of us was born into a family on earth. If we are sealed to our families and remain righteous, we can return to live with them and with Heavenly Father and Jesus Christ again.

Everything we need as spiritual beings, regardless of which sphere we are living in—premortal life, earth life, and beyond—is found within the family system. How we exist, learn, grow, and experience life all spring from this basic unit called the family. Indeed, the whole plan of salvation is encapsulated within family life.

OUR MORTAL EXPERIENCE ON EARTH

In many ways our earth life mirrors our pre-earth life. We still have our agency. We can still grow and develop. We still receive guidance and direction from our Heavenly Father and our Savior, Jesus Christ. We have talents and gifts we can discover and magnify.

As part of Heavenly Father's plan, the family is a place for children to learn and progress in the gospel, just as we did as spirits in the pre-earth life. Joseph B. Wirthlin of the Quorum of the Twelve Apostles reminds us of that truth: "In the plan of salvation, all families are precious instruments in the Lord's hands to help direct His children toward a celestial destination. The righteous molding of an immortal soul is the highest work we can do, and the home is the place to do it. To accomplish this eternal work, we should make our homes gospel centered" (Wirthlin 1993).

Families exist on a continuum of spiritual health, ranging from spiritually broken and filled with darkness, all the way to spiritually whole and full of God's light. Most families fall somewhere in the middle, with mistakes made and deep hurts inflicted. There is no perfect parent on earth. This is a learn-as-you go job. President Spencer W. Kimball stated: "My brothers and sisters, we're away from home. We're off to school. Our lessons will not be easy. The way we react to them, the way we conquer and accomplish and live will determine our rewards, and they will be permanent and eternal. . . . You are sent to this world with a very serious purpose. You are sent to school, for that matter, to begin as a human infant and grow to unbelievable proportions in wisdom, judgment, knowledge, and power" (Kimball 1982, 28, 31).

Even the role of a parent is part of our "education," and we rarely get straight A's. One reason it is so difficult to be a good parent is that we live in a fallen and mortal state. There is death. There is evil. Our spirits reside inside of physical bodies that are flawed and that will eventually die. How we learn, progress, think, and feel is all filtered through the body. Therefore, our thought processes can become twisted and distorted. Our emotions can seem overwhelming and crippling. We can struggle with learning disorders, mental and emotional problems, and even disease. The cravings and appetites of our physical bodies can be experienced as very strong and can lead to debilitating addictions, destroying us physically and spiritually.

When we are raised by a wounded, broken mother or father, we are often affected by his or her baggage. Indeed, it is becoming rarer and rarer to escape childhood without emotional and spiritual wounds. So, when we become parents, our wounds are often magnified and become stumbling blocks to creating a home life that is safe, secure, and full of love.

CHARITY-BASED PARENTING

Codependency is Satan's counterfeit to charity. Parenting from that dysfunctional place causes our children to believe this is the way Christ would act, that our codependent behaviors are a reflection of pure love. Living this lie will only produce one thing—a stumbling block to finding Christ, to experiencing His power, mercy, and love.

So, what does effective, charity-based, codependently sober parenting look like? The following chart shows how Christ-centered parenting is directly opposite from codependent-based parenting. Which category do you fall under?

Charity Is:

Long-Suffering

- Allow your child time to grasp concepts, to learn from his or her mistakes.
- Be patient with your child as he or she learns new skills.
- Treat yourself with patience and compassion. Forgive yourself. Let go of self-hatred and rigid, extreme expectations. You can't offer patience and compassion to your child if you don't have it for yourself.

Kind

- Hold your child accountable, but acknowledge how hard it is for him or her.
- Do what the child wants for a change.
- Find ways to say yes.
- Take a moment to stop what you are doing and get on your child's level to listen and play.
- Meet your child's needs. Make it safe for the child to express his or her needs.
- Don't beat yourself up. Be gentle with yourself. Look to God for comfort.

Envieth Not

- Don't compare your damaged, harsh, or poor childhood with your child's experience. Don't get angry about it. Don't throw it in your child's face and say, "You got it so good," trying to make the child feel guilty or ashamed for the things he or she has.
- Promote gratitude. Recognize the blessings you receive from God in your own life.

Not Puffed Up

- No double standard—"You have to apologize, but I do not, because I'm the adult and you're the kid," or "Rated-R movies are okay for us to watch, but not you," or "I can skip church because I'm tired, but you have to go."
- Don't brag about your children to others to make yourself or the family look better.
- It's okay to admit parenting mistakes to your child. It helps the child learn how to handle his or her future mistakes and shortcomings.

Seeketh Not Her Own

- Play with kids instead of disconnecting (distractions, addictions). Don't be selfish and self-centered.

- Don't take credit for your child's success to build your own self esteem. It won't work and you'll be living through the child instead of living your own life. Your child will come to resent you for it, and you'll come to resent him or her for not being perfect.
- Don't say, "I'll meet my child's needs or wishes, but it has to be done on my terms."

Not Easily Provoked

- Avoid acting from a place where the child is seen as a threat to your power—your position in the family. Don't demand respect (fear based); instead, foster an atmosphere of love and respect towards others. Respect will come from family members as a natural outgrowth of feeling validated and supported.
- Don't yell about spilled milk. In other words, don't sweat the small stuff.
- Don't take your child's temper tantrums personally. Don't blame your child when you lose control of your anger.
- Remember that if you are easily provoked, it is often because you are operating from a place of insecurity, seeing yourself as less than or not enough.

Thinketh No Evil

- No conspiracy theories. Sometimes what is happening is exactly what it looks like.
- Don't future trip, making the future out to be worst-case scenario. "I just know Johnny will crash the car," or "Johnny is going to flunk math this year."
- Give your child the benefit of the doubt. Don't be naive, but don't be quick to accuse, either.
- Don't find ways for your child to gratify your personal needs.

Rejoiceth Not in Iniquity

- Don't teach evil practices (lying, cheating, stealing, putting others down, etc.).
- Don't teach dysfunctional coping skills. Do all you can to overcome your own codependency traits and patterns so that they don't get passed along to your child.
- Set and enforce standards.
- Encourage your child to be positive, good, and responsible.

Rejoiceth in Truth

- Act congruently—make sure your inside matches your outside. Help your child to trust that who you are won't change no matter where you are or who you are with. Be authentic. If you feel sad, show sadness. If you feel scared, show it. It will help your child be more in tune with himself or herself.

- Be self-aware. Promote an atmosphere where your child feels safe to reflect and become aware of his or her thoughts, feelings, and beliefs.
- Have personal integrity, making your actions match your beliefs. Encourage your child to stand up for what is right by doing it yourself.
- Enjoy wholesome, good things.
- Encourage scripture reading by doing it yourself.
- Bear your testimony to your child.

Beareth All Things

- Bear your own sorrow and pain in life and don't put it on your child to carry.
- Allow your child to see your weaknesses. Be open and teach your child the process of change.
- Be humble.

Believeth All Things

- "I can do all things with God's help."
- Encourage faith. Show trust in yourself, each other, and God. Your child won't trust God if he or she can't trust you.

Hopeth All Things

- Be optimistic.
- Work on not becoming easily discouraged.
- Hand your anxiety over to the Lord.
- If you struggle with depression, work to manage and take care of it. Your child will see you as unavailable if you remain stuck in your depression.

Endureth All Things

- Endure your children's mistakes and the consequences of those mistakes. "I won't reject you because of your imperfectness."
- Teach your child that your love will never fade, end, or leave. Your love for your child must endure all the silly, petty, immature, or rebellious things he or she will do. That doesn't mean you turn a blind eye to what the child is doing, or that you should put up with unsafe behavior. It means you never stop showing your love.
- Support your child in his or her healthy decisions. Don't support him or her in unhealthy decisions. That would be enabling, and it will do your child no favors.

Even when a parent works through his or her own issues, there is no guarantee that his or her children will remain true to the faith. Why? Because the children still have their agency. President James E. Faust explained: "Our agency, given us through the plan of our Father, is the great alternative to Satan's plan of force. With this sublime gift, we can grow, improve, progress, and seek perfection. Without agency, none of us could grow and develop by learning from our mistakes and errors and those of others" (Faust 2007).

Giving a child agency as he or she learns and grows is scary. There is great potential for the child to make poor choices and get hurt. So, what do we do? We teach, but we do not compel. We love, but we do not smother. We have firm boundaries, but we do not use force. We guide, but we do not dictate. We ask our children to follow our example, not just our words. As Dayton writes, "Much of parenting is implicit rather than explicit, which is why children become who we are rather than who we tell them to be" (Dayton 2007, 136).

We counsel, but we do not order. We live the gospel, but we do not coerce or constrain our children to do likewise. Just as Father in Heaven will never push or shove His children into heaven, we as earthly parents need to allow our children to exercise their agency.

Let us not forget who these children are that we are raising. Elder Bruce R. McConkie declared: "A child is an adult spirit in a newly born body, a body capable of growing and maturing according to the plan of Him whose spirit children we all are. Children are the sons and daughters of God. They lived and dwelt with him for eons before their mortal birth. They are adults before birth; they are adults at death" (McConkie 1977).

The pain and suffering, the grief and worry, the countless prayers, the sleepless nights—being a parent can stretch your heartstrings to the very limit. When a son or daughter chooses a path that leads to darkness and destruction, that pain can become almost unbearable. In these moments, agency can be seen as a damning device rather than a freeing gift from God.

In our pain, in our fear for our children, we can easily slip into using methods that are not Christlike. Manipulation, guilt trips, using shame to produce desired outcomes, using force or coercion or threats or ultimatums—all end up binding us in chains just as much as the child's own choices have bound him or her in chains.

Any time we seek to limit someone else's agency, we end up limiting our own. At that point we have become followers of Satan, seeking to implement his plan within the confines of our homes. It doesn't matter how righteous a cause it is (even Lucifer may have had a certain amount of goodwill—with his plan, no one would be lost). The sacrifice of losing agency appeared to be worth it if everyone would make it back, right? Wrong. Elder Larry W. Wilson taught: "We lose our right to the Lord's Spirit . . . when we exercise control over another person in an unrighteous manner. We may think such methods are for the good of the one being 'controlled.' But any time we try to compel someone to righteousness who can and should be exercising his or her own moral agency, we are acting unrighteously" (Wilson 2012).

LOVE THE LOST CHILD

The way in which Nephi dealt with his brothers is a pattern for how we might treat a wayward son or daughter. Elder Allan E. Bergin taught: "There is another virtue in Nephi's character that has always been compelling to me. He did not emotionally cut off his brothers; that is, he seems not to have held grudges. Love followed rebuke and exhortation. We sense some of his sorrow when his brothers rejected the invitation to embrace the gospel of Jesus Christ. 'I did frankly forgive them all that they had done,' he says of his early life (1 Ne. 7:21), and years later he wrote, 'I pray continually for them by day, and mine eyes water my pillow by night, because of them' (2 Ne. 33:3)" (Bergin 1976).

Our premortal family is the example of how to handle family situations here on earth. Was there a chance to grow and develop? Yes. Did our Heavenly Parents allow us to pursue our hearts' desires? Yes. Did we have agency in this first family? Yes. Were there family rules that were enforced? Yes. Were there arguments, dissension, and even open rebellion in our first family? Yes. The scriptures described that rebellion as a "war" (see Revelation 12:7). And how did Heavenly Father react to that rebellion? With love. Yes, even the Father showed his love for the fallen, wayward son. President James E. Faust explained:

> *Because of his rebellion, Lucifer was cast out and "became Satan, yea, even the devil, the father of all lies, to deceive and to blind men, and to lead them captive at his will, even as many as would not hearken unto [the Lord's] voice." And so this personage who was an angel of God and in authority, even in the presence of God, was removed from the presence of God and His Son. This caused great sadness, "for the heavens wept over him—he was Lucifer, a son of the morning." Does this not place some responsibility on the followers of Christ to show concern for loved ones who have lost their way and "are shut out from the presence of God"? I know of no*

better way than to show unconditional love to help lost souls seek another path."
(Faust 2007)

THE TWELVE STEPS FOR PARENTS

The LDS Addiction Recovery Program uses the twelve steps of recovery to help us access the Atonement and overcome our addictions and compulsions. Within those steps are principles that help us gain codependent sobriety and practice charity-based parenting. We'll end this chapter by reviewing these steps, plugging in our parenting issues.

Step 1. Admitted we were powerless over the choices our children have made and that our lives have become unmanageable trying to control them.

Step 2. Come to believe that the power of God can restore us and our children to complete spiritual health.

Step 3. Decide to turn our wills and our lives and our children over to the care of God the Eternal Father and His Son, Jesus Christ.

Step 4. Make a searching and fearless written moral inventory of our behaviors as parents.

Step 5. Admit to ourselves; to our Heavenly Father, in the name of Jesus Christ; to proper priesthood authority as necessary; and to another couple the exact nature of our parenting wrongs.

Step 6. Become entirely ready to have God remove all our parenting weaknesses.

Step 7. Humbly ask Heavenly Father to remove our parenting shortcomings.

Step 8. Make a written list of all family members we have harmed and become willing to make restitution to them.

Step 9. Whenever possible, make direct amends to the family members we have harmed.

Step 10. Continue to take personal inventory of our parenting techniques, and when we are wrong, promptly admit it.

Step 11. Seek through prayer and meditation to know the Lord's will in how we should parent our children and to have the power to carry it out.

Step 12. Having had a spiritual awakening as a result of the Atonement of Jesus Christ, share this message with other parents, and practice these principles in all you do.

PART 6

WRITTEN EXERCISES

The Church's twelve-step program assists people in overcoming addictions and other maladaptive behaviors by using the Atonement of Jesus Christ. The next three chapters will help the codependent Latter-day Saint start his or her twelve-step journey. These beginning steps will offer the recovering codependent the foundation needed to apply the Atonement.

STEP 1 EXERCISES

STEP 1: ADMIT THAT YOU ARE POWERLESS OVER YOUR CODEPENDENCY AND THAT YOUR LIFE HAS BECOME UNMANAGEABLE.

Step 1 helps us to understand and become aware of the following:

More than anything else, codependency is created out of a need to control fear. What are your fears? Are you afraid of love or loneliness or being abandoned? Are you afraid of being seen as inferior or less than? Are you afraid of others seeing you as powerless? Are you afraid of the dark, of death, of Judgment Day? Are you afraid God won't be there for you when you really need Him? Are you afraid of getting hurt again, of being let down, ignored, or rejected?

Point C
Willfulness—playing God. Going after my will always causes
suffering for myself and my loved ones

Codependent Safety
(safety based on my power)
This type of safety is always
elusive—have to always be on guard.
Survival is, by necessity, always selfish.
Survival is not living—no room for
emotions. I must become a "doer," robotic.
**Fear is the motivator, the engine and
motor of this triangle.** The more I travel this
triangle, the more fruit it will bear and the
more entrenched and trapped I will become.

Starting Point A
Faulty beliefs:
* There is nobody else to keep me safe.
* I can't trust anyone.
* If I am good enough, strong enough,
  then God will help me.

Point B
Seek for control/power

1. After you review an example from Tanni, a group member, write down your own answers in the space provided.

WHAT ARE MY FEARS?	HOW I HANDLE MY FEARS (BEHAVIORS)
Rejection	Never say no. Be an overachiever. Find out what someone wants and give it to him or her.
Remembering the traumatic past	Be really busy—overinvolved. Overload my plate. Take on more than I can handle.
That it is true—I'm worthless	Be a superachiever. Constantly help other people.
Anger, rage	Keep people happy. Be the people pleaser, the "buffer" between others.
That in the end, I will be alone/ abandoned	Create a façade of always being happy, outgoing. Inside I may be empty and depressed, but I will never let anyone know that.

WHAT ARE MY FEARS?	HOW I HANDLE MY FEARS (BEHAVIORS)

2. Since step 1 is about seeing our powerlessness over our codependency, let's take your list of behaviors (exercise 1, above), the things you do to try to handle your fears. Write them in a list by themselves under the heading "What My Codependency Looks Like."

_____

_____

_____

_____

_____

3. If you are having trouble completing the exercises, read the following list adapted from Charlotte Kasl's book *Women, Sex, and Addiction* (1990, 31–42, 151–69). Place a check mark next to the sentences that apply to you.

- ☐ I am powerless to stop taking personally all the words and actions of those around me.
- ☐ I am powerless to get angry when someone violates my boundaries. I can't stand up for myself.
- ☐ I am powerless to say no.
- ☐ I am powerless to let people suffer with their own problems and take responsibility for themselves. I have to step in. I can't help myself. I am overwhelmed at their expressions of pain and hurt. I have to rescue them, or at least try.
- ☐ I am powerless to help my children build their self-esteem by pushing them to excel. Doing x, y, or z will make them feel good about themselves. I will accept nothing short of perfection for my children.
- ☐ I am powerless to stop trying to change my spouse. I find myself saying, "Wouldn't you like to . . ." or "Don't you think you should . . ." or "Wouldn't it be nice if you . . ."
- ☐ I am powerless to stop worrying constantly over other people or experiences.
- ☐ I am powerless to face life on my own. I need to be needed and have to have someone by my side.
- ☐ I am powerless to make up and create my own sense of self. How I feel about me, what I see in me, comes from you. You tell me who and what I am.
- ☐ I am powerless to stop putting on that façade that everything is okay, or that I am perfect, or that nothing bothers me, etc.

4. Once you finish the above list, answer this question: How does being codependent offer you a short-term fix? Come up with at least three examples.

_____

_____

_____

5. Kasl wrote: "Rationalization is a cue signaling that you are off center, that you want something to be the way it isn't. The codependent spends an enormous amount of time 'in her [his] head,' rationalizing life, trying to figure out how to make an impossible situation work" (ibid 56–57). Come up with at least five "hooks" or rationalizations you use to jump into your codependent behavior. For example: "But they need my help," or "They are not doing it right," or "My heart breaks in two watching him (or her) struggle."

_____

_____

_____

6. Come up with at least three examples of you trying to control something or someone that was uncontrollable.

_____

_____

_____

7. Come up with three examples of when your codependency took you to the brink of exhaustion mentally, emotionally, and physically.

_____

_____

_____

8. Write down ten consequences that have come to you because of your codependent behavior. Specifically, review how it has damaged your relationships with others, how has it impacted your sense of worth, how it has distorted your perception, and how has it affected your spirituality.

_____

_____

_____

_____

_____

_____

_____

_____

_____

_____

10. Write down at least five examples or snapshots of yourself in your prideful state. This is often a hard thing to see. In working with Nate, a recovering Latter-day Saint, we came up with a list of possible indicators that a person is in a prideful state:

- Closing off
- Avoiding spouse and others
- Short-tempered
- Feeling hopeless
- Being angry without cause
- Rejecting help
- Arguing just to prove I'm right
- Not wanting to pray or read the scriptures (I don't want to, I don't need to)
- Not being able to hear or accept feedback
- When faults are pointed out, turn the spotlight back on the other person
- Wanting to skip Church meetings on Sunday, as well as other Church meetings
- Focusing on faults of others
- Preachy
- Self-righteous (secret judging, condemning, comparing)

_____

_____

_____

_____

_____

11. Answer this question: What happens when I put my faith in me versus putting it in God? How do I feel?

_____

_____

_____

12. Write down five examples of you needing to be in control.

_____

_____

_____

_____

_____

13. Answer this question: How do you feel when you are not in control?

_____

_____

_____

14. Write a letter to someone—God, yourself, your spouse, the Savior—about why you want to recover/repent and become sober and abstinent from your codependency. If you need more space, use a notebook.

_____

_____

_____

_____

_____

_____

_____

_____

Step 2 Exercises

Step 2: Come to believe that the power of God can restore you to complete spiritual health.

Steps 2 and 3 help the recovering codependent understand the following doctrines and application of those truths:

Point C

Love. Receiving love requires trust. Without trust, love cannot flourish. Without trust, we return to our coping skills to keep us safe. We close our hearts to love. Giving love (without my will directing it) and receiving love is necessary for charity to exist

True Safety

Trust, surrendering my will and love, creates true safety. All are essential points needed to create lasting safety. In this state of Heaven-sent protection, lasting change can be experienced. Grace is the motivator, the engine—the power behind moving from point to point in the triangle. The more one lives in this triangle, the more fruit it will bear. The more at peace I will be, the more free I will be, the more optimistic I will be, the more faith I will have.

Starting Point A

Trusting God. I need to know God in order to trust Him (see Mosiah 5:12–13). Then I can be vulnerable with Him and open up myself to feel His love.

Point B

Surrendering my will. This looks like having a broken heart and a contrite spirit. It looks like acceptance, humility, submissiveness.

As codependents move from step 1, their new awareness of their powerlessness and unmanageability can deplete the hope they are clinging to. That despair can become so great that it erodes faith. It can even cause us to feel abandoned by God.

Yet with time and diligence and prayer, hope begins to blossom again—or in some cases, for the first time. Hope builds an anchor we can hold onto in the midst of chaos. "Wherefore, whoso believeth in God might with surety hope for a better world, yea, even a place at the right hand of God, which hope cometh of faith, maketh an anchor to the souls of men, which would make them sure and steadfast, always abounding in good works, being led to glorify God" (Ether 12:4). Self-will can be replaced with trust in the love and power of Jesus Christ.

1. Write down what it has done to your self-esteem and self-worth to constantly let yourself down—to be unable to be perfect, unable to juggle fifteen balls in the air, unable to get your spouse/child/friend to change, unable to keep people happy.

   _____
   _____
   _____

2. When do you feel hopeless?

   _____
   _____
   _____

3. When do you feel overwhelmed and powerless?

   _____
   _____
   _____

4. How do you end up dealing with hopelessness, powerlessness, and feeling overwhelmed?

   _____
   _____
   _____

5. What do you think the adversary does with your fears?

_____

_____

_____

6. How do these fears affect your faith? (Review the list about your fears from step 1.)

_____

_____

_____

7. What impact do you think your childhood wounds have had on your spirituality?

_____

_____

_____

8. Write about what comes to mind when you read the following phrase: "Step 2 is where God becomes bigger than my fears/insecurities."

_____

_____

_____

9. How do you act codependent with God? Here is an example to get you started: "I will make Heavenly Father love me by doing . . ."

_____

_____

_____

10. Come up with a sketch of what codependent sobriety looks like for you. If you are going to believe that God can restore you to complete spiritual health, you need to be able to at least have a sense or idea of what that might look like. Charlotte Kasl offers a glimpse as to what codependent sobriety looks like. The following sketches are adapted from her book *Women, Sex, and Addiction* (Kasl 1990, 332–54). Place a check mark next to the ones that fit for you. Then plug in your own examples.

Twelve Signs of Codependent Sobriety

- [ ] Give no advice. Resist the temptation to tell or hint to other people what is best for them. Interrupt yourself every time you start to think about how you'd like someone else to change. Ask yourself, "What do I need to do for me right now?"

- [ ] Think no advice. Tell your mind to listen quietly and respectfully or to observe others with curiosity. Codependents usually find their minds racing with thoughts about what others should do. Sobriety is when you are so totally in someone's presence and in the present moment that when suddenly asked for advice, you have to rely on your Higher Power to give it to you.

- [ ] Stop telling stories that could be titled *What He/She Did to Me.* Telling these stories keeps you in the victim role. People who tell lengthy stories about what others did to them often do so in order to keep friends—the unspoken goal is for the friend to say, "Oh, poor you, that is really terrible." Blaming others creates dense energy and is one of the greatest stumbling blocks to recovery. Instead, learn to take responsibility for your feelings by saying, "I am angry at _____ for _____."

- [ ] Stop listening to your friends tell stories of what their partners did to them. When you encourage your friends to tell you their "victim stories" in order to create a bond between you, you are creating a codependent-based friendship.

- [ ] Stop giving reasons for everything you do. Stop using the word *because.* Codependents tend to feel the need to justify themselves. Learn to say, "I want to go to that movie," not "I want to go to that movie because . . ."

- [ ] Take your emotional temperature after visiting with others. On a scale of 1 to 10, how did you feel before and after visiting with this person? Become aware of what brings light into your life and what brings dense feelings into your life.

- [ ] Change the question "Will they like me?" to "Will I like them?" Most codependents think, "Will anyone like me?" This puts a person in the victim role.

- [ ] Learn to keep your energy inside. Codependents often feel their energy spill out when another person walks into the room or spends an evening with them.

- [ ] Pay attention to behavior, not words. Codependents are easily seduced by words. Behavior is the true measure of a person. Just because someone says "I love you" doesn't mean it is so.

- [ ] Let relationships find their own level. Codependents typically put more energy into relationships than their partners or friends do. This just leaves the codependent feeling irritated, exhausted, and ripped off.
- [ ] Anything besides yes means no.
- [ ] Become powerful rather than being self-righteous and feeling superior to others. This is the high codependents feel when they are being self-righteous and judging others as wrong or stupid. This is tough to give up because this superior stance brings a feeling of power. Codependents put down others to hide their shame about being dishonest, dependent, or jealous.
- [ ] Other specific changes in your own life that prove you are being sober from your codependency:

_____

_____

_____

_____

_____

_____

STEP 3 EXERCISES

STEP 3: DECIDE TO TURN YOUR WILL AND YOUR LIFE OVER TO THE CARE OF GOD THE ETERNAL FATHER AND HIS SON, JESUS CHRIST.

Step 3 helps us surrender our willfulness, thus allowing us to experience the care, protection, and love of our Heavenly Father.

Exhibiting various forms of control and acting on hidden and secret motivations creates more chaos—more unmanageability. Trying to control or manipulate others is frustrating and exhausting. "It blocks other people's ability to grow. . . . It doesn't matter if they're hurting themselves. It doesn't matter if we could help them if only they'd listen to and cooperate with us. . . .We cannot change people. Any attempts to control them are a delusion as well as an illusion" (Healing 18).

Letting go of our will, of doing it our way, and turning to God leads to peace, growth, and strength. This step builds on the trust developed in step 2. Now we can turn our own lives over to God's care, trusting He won't let go of us and that He will do for our loved ones what we could never do—save them from themselves.

Answer the following questions:

1. Why do you go to church? What are your motives? Is there anyone besides yourself that is "making" you go? If so, what would it take for you to want to go?

   _____

   _____

   _____

   _____

   _____

2. If you do want to go to church, what are thoughts that try to stop you from going?

   _____

   _____

   _____

   _____

   _____

3. What does it feel like when you open up and become vulnerable? What do you do to avoid feeling vulnerable?

_____

_____

_____

4. Write down as many excuses as you can in four minutes about why it's hard to let go of your will.

_____

_____

_____

_____

_____

_____

_____

_____

_____

5. What do you see in those excuses?

_____

_____

_____

6. How can you overcome these thoughts?

_____

_____

_____

7. For three days, try the following experiment: Dedicate yourself to God's will at the start of each day. At the beginning of each hour, take a quiet moment and say: "I surrender my will to Thee, Father, and dedicate myself to following Thee and the Savior. May I feel Thy strength and power and receive inspiration to help me submit to Thee." What happened?

_____

_____

_____

_____

_____

8. Memorize the Serenity Prayer (see page 177) and recite it when you want to take back control.

9. Read the story of Alma the Elder in Mosiah 23–24.

How does this story relate to your struggle with codependency?

_____

_____

_____

How does this account help you to give up control and submit to the Lord?

_____

_____

_____

Scriptures to Encourage You to Let Go of Your Will

- 2 Nephi 9:10—The Lord "prepareth a way for our escape."
- 1 Nephi 4:3—"The Lord is able to deliver us."
- Mosiah 9:14–18—"He [God] did deliver us."
- 1 Corinthians 10:13—The Lord will "make a way to escape."
- Mormon 9:19—"God is a God of miracles."
- 1 Nephi 17: 31—"And according to his word he did lead them; and according to his word he did do all things for them."
- 1 Nephi 3:7—"[God] shall prepare a way for them that they may accomplish the thing which he commandeth them." Are there other scriptures you can find that prove God will take care of you as you let go of your will?

THE SERENITY PRAYER

God, grant me the serenity
To accept the things I cannot change;
Courage to change the things I can;
And wisdom to know the difference.

Living one day at a time;
Enjoying one moment at a time;
Accepting hardships as the pathway to peace;
Taking, as He did, this sinful world
As it is, not as I would have it.

Trusting that He will make all things right
If I surrender to His will,
That I may be reasonably happy in this life
And supremely happy with Him forever in the next.
Amen.

Reference List

Ballard, M. Russell. 2010. "O That Cunning Plan." *Ensign*, Nov. Salt Lake City, UT: The Church of Jesus Christ of Latter-day Saints.

Beattie, Melody. 1992. *Codependent No More: How to Stop Controlling Others and Start Caring for Yourself.* Center City, MN: Hazelden Publishing.

Bennion, Lowell L. 1981. "Overcoming Our Mistakes." *Ensign,* July.

Benson, Ezra T. 1988. "Jesus Christ—Gifts and Expectations. *Ensign,* Dec.

Bergin, Allen E. 1976. "Nephi, a Universal Man," *Ensign,* Sept.

Black, Claudia. 2002. *Changing Course: Healing from Loss, Abandonment and Fear.* 2nd ed. Center City, MN: Hazelden Publishing.

Bowlby, John Edward. 1983. *Attachment and Loss, Volume 1: Attachment.* 2nd ed. New York City: Basic Books.

Brennan, Kelly A., Catherine L. Clark, and Phillip R. Shaver. 1998. "Self-Report Measurement of Adult Attachment and Romantic Relationships: An Integrative Overview." In Simpson, J. A., and Rholes, W. S., eds. *Attachment Theory and Close Relationships* (46–76). New York City: Guilford Press.

Burney, Robert. 1995. *Codependence: The Dance of Wounded Souls.* Encinitas, CA: Joy to You & Me Enterprises.

Burton, Linda K. 2013. "First Observe, Then Serve*." Ensign,* May.

Carnes, Patrick. 1997. *Sexual Anorexia: Overcoming Sexual Self-Hatred.* Center City, MN: Hazelden.

Cohen, Sheldon. 2004. "Social Relationships and Health." *American Psychologist* 59:676–84.

Cook, Gene R. 2002. "Charity: Perfect and Everlasting Love." *Ensign,* May.

Dayton, Tian. 2007. *Emotional Sobriety: From Relationship Trauma to Resilience and Balance.* Deerfield Beach, FL: Health Communications, Inc.

Erying, Henry B. 2012. "Mountains to Climb." *Ensign,* May.

Faust, James E. 2007. "The Forces That Will Save Us." *Ensign,* May.

Fraley, R. Chris, and George A. Bonanno. 2004. "Attachment and Loss: A Test of Three Competing Models on the Association between Attachment-Related Avoidance and Adaptation to Bereavement." *Personality and Social Psychology Bulletin* 30(7): 878–90.

Hales, Robert D. 2012. "Being a More Christian Christian." *Ensign,* Nov.

Healing Through Christ Institute. 2013. *Healing Through Christ.* Version 1.3. St. George, UT: Healing Through Christ Institute.

Holland, Jeffrey R. 2003. *Trusting Jesus.* Salt Lake City, UT: Deseret Book Co.

Kasl, Charlotte. 1990. *Women, Sex, and Addiction: A Search for Love and Power.* New York City: William Morrow and Company.

———. 2001. *If the Buddha Married: Creating Enduring Relationships on a Spiritual Path.* New York City: Penguin Books.

Kimball, Spencer W. 1982. *The Teachings of Spencer W. Kimball: Twelfth President of the Church of Jesus Christ of Latter-day Saints.* Edited by Edward L. Kimball. Salt Lake City, UT: Bookcraft.

LDS Family Services Addiction Recovery Program. 2005. *A Guide to Addiction Recovery and Healing.* Salt Lake City, UT: The Church of Jesus Christ of Latter-day Saints.

Lee, Harold B. 1971. "The Way to Eternal Life." *Ensign,* Nov.

McConkie, Bruce R. 1977. "The Salvation of Little Children." *Ensign,* May.

Mellody, Pia. 2002. "Boundaries." Lecture presented at The Meadows, Wickenburg, AZ.

———. 2003. *Facing Codependence: What It Is, Where It Comes from, How It Sabotages Our Lives*. New York City: Harper & Row.

Money, John. 1986. *Lovemaps: Clinical Concepts of Sexual/Erotic Health and Pathology, Paraphilia, and Gender Transposition in Childhood, Adolescence, and Maturity.* Buffalo, NY: Prometheus Books.

Muller, Robert T., Lisa A. Sicoli, and Kathryn Lemieux. 2000. "Attachment Style and Posttraumatic Stress Symptomatology among Adults Who Report the Experience of Childhood Abuse." *Journal of Traumatic Stress* 13:321–32.

Newman, Mildred, and Bernard Berkowitz. 1986. *How to Be Your Own Best Friend.* New York City: Ballantine Books.

Oaks, Dallin H. 1985. "Spirituality." *Ensign,* Nov.

O'Mara, Peggy. 1993. *The Way Back Home: Essays on Life and Family.* New York City: Mothering (Simon & Schuster).

Porter, Lauren L. 2003. "The Science of Attachment: The Biological Roots of Love." *Mothering,* July/August.

Pratt, Parley P. 2012. *Key to the Science of Theology.* Classic Reprint Series. Hong Kong: Forgotten Books. Originally published in 1855 by F. D. Richards (Liverpool) and Latter Day Saints Book Depot (London).

Prior, Stephen. 1996. *Object Relations in Severe Trauma: Psychotherapy of the Sexually Abused Child.* Lanham, MD: Jason Aronson, Inc.

Punamäki, Raija-Leena. 2002. "The Uninvited Guest of War Enters Childhood: Developmental and Personality Aspects of War and Military Violence." *Traumatology* 8:181.

Robbins, Lynn G. 2011."What Manner of Men and Women Ought Ye to Be?" *Ensign,* May.

Romney, Marion G. 1971. "Satan—The Great Deceiver." *Ensign,* June.

Ross, Colin. 2002. "Self-Blame and Addiction." *Paradigm* 7, no. 2 (Spring 2002): 14–18.

Schaeffer, Brenda. 1986. *Power Plays* (pamphlet). Healthy Relationships Series. Center City, MN: Hazelden Publishing & Educational Services.

———. 2009. *Is It Love, or Is It Addiction?* 3rd ed. Center City, MN: Hazelden Publishing.

Shahar, Charles. 2006. "The Martyr-Victim Complex Described." http://www.yourlifecheckup. com/article.php?artid=65.

Smith, George Albert, and Preston Nibley. 1948. *Sharing the Gospel with Others.* Salt Lake City: Deseret Book Co.

Smith, Joseph, Oliver Cowdery, Sidney Rigdon, and Frederick G. Williams, comp. 2010. *Lectures on Faith: Delivered to the School of the Prophets in Kirtland, Ohio, 1834–35.* Springville, UT: Cedar Fort, Inc. Originally published in 1835 in The Doctrine and Covenants of the Church of the Latter Day Saints, in Kirtland, Ohio.

Smith, Joseph F. 1948. In Daniel H. Ludlow, comp. *Latter-day Prophets: Selections from the Sermons and Writings of Church Presidents.* Salt Lake City, UT: Deseret Book Co.

Snow, Eliza R. 1874. "An Address by Miss Eliza R. Snow." *The Latter-day Saints Millennial Star,* Jan. 13.

Uchtdorf, Dieter F. 2006. "See the End from the Beginning." *Ensign,* May.

———. 2011. "Forget Me Not," *Ensign,* Nov.

———. 2013. "Four Titles." *Ensign,* May.

Vogel, Miriam. 1994. "Gender as a Factor in the Transgenerational Transmission of Trauma." *Women & Therapy* 15(2): 35–47.

Wasson, Nancy. 2006. "Is There a Martyr in Your Marriage?" http://www.ezinepost.com/ articles/article-51423.html.

Weinhold, Janae, and Barry Weinhold. 2008. *Breaking Free of the CoDependency Trap.* 2nd ed. Novato, CA: New World Library.

Wilson, Larry W. 2012. "Only upon the Principles of Righteousness." *Ensign,* May.

Wirthlin, Joseph B. 1993. "Spiritually Strong Homes and Families." *Ensign,* May.

Whitfield, Charles. 1994. *Boundaries and Relationships: Knowing, Protecting and Enjoying the Self.* Deerfield Beach, FL: Health Communications, Inc.

Whitney, Orson F. 1955. Quoted in Spencer W. Kimball. *Faith Precedes the Miracle.* Salt Lake City, UT: Deseret Book Co.

Wolinski, Stephen. 1991. *Trances People Live.* Wilton Manors, FL: Bramble Books.

ABOUT THE AUTHOR

Douglas Dobberfuhl was born and raised in northwestern Wisconsin, where the snow was deep and the summers were humid. As a child, he could be found at the local swimming pool or immersed in a book. Doug served a full-time LDS Church mission in Brussels, Belgium. When he came home, he attended Brigham Young University. During his first semester at BYU, he met his future wife, Stephanie. She got his attention during a food fight at the Deseret Towers cafeteria. They were married six months later in the Los Angeles Temple.

Doug received a masters of science degree in marriage and family therapy from Nova Southeastern University. He has worked as a counselor for twenty years. He has been a clinical supervisor, offered home-based counseling, done outpatient as well as inpatient work, and is the founder of The LDS Center for Trauma Resolution and Addiction Recovery (LDS-CRR) in Vancouver, Washington.

Doug also wrote *Overcoming Addiction: The Journey Begins* and *Overcoming Addiction: A Twelve-Step Companion Guide*. He has been a contributing editor for *SheUnlimited* online magazine, a woman's health and wellness periodical, as well as for *A Second Opinion*, a health and holistic-healing magazine. He is the author of *Using Scrapbooking to Heal from Childhood Trauma*, as well as many articles for treatment centers, including "Sexually Reactive Female Adolescents: Theory and Case Study," and "Intellectualizing: Denying Emotional States." Doug and his wife Stephanie have five children.